Chakras

Made Easy

Chakras

Made Easy

Seven Keys to Awakening and Healing the Energy Body

ANODEA JUDITH

HAY HOUSE

Carlsbad, California • New York City
London • Sydney • New Delhi

Published in the United States by:
Hay House LLC: www.hayhouse.com˚

Published in Australia by:
Hay House Australia Ltd.: www.hayhouse.com.au

Published in the United Kingdom by:
Hay House UK Ltd.: www.hayhouse.co.uk

Published in India by:
Hay House Publishers India: www.hayhouse.co.in

Text © Anodea Judith, 2016

The moral rights of the author have been asserted.

This book was previously published as *Chakras* (*Hay
House Basics* series); ISBN: 978-1-78180-709-5

A catalogue record for this book is available from the British Library.

Interior illustrations: iii, vii, ix, 1, 193, 199 Thinkstock; 16 Mary Ann Zapalac;
25, 40, 61, 80, 102, 106, 123, 151, 171, Shanon Dean;
All other artwork by Alex Wayne, adapted by Shanon Dean

ISBN: 978-1-78817-250-9

16 15 14 13 12 11 10 9 8 7

Printed in the United States of America

This product uses responsibly sourced papers and/or recycled
materials. For more information, see www.hayhouse.com.

*To the infinite possibilities that lie along
the bridge between heaven and Earth*

Contents

List of Exercises

The Journey Begins

We're all on a journey. A journey to heal ourselves, to figure out what life's all about, to discover the deeper mysteries. It's a challenging journey with fits and starts, dead-ends, and confusing choices. Things happen to us and we lose our way. We wake up later, asking, "Now where was I going before all *that* happened?"

Wouldn't it be nice if someone gave you a guidebook? Or at least a map?

The chakra system is exactly that – *a map for the journey through life.* This is a guidebook for that journey. It's based upon seven spinning wheels of energy that act as gears, moving your vehicle along its path. Using this map not only helps you find your way along life's journey, but also makes the journey worthwhile. It is a map to full-spectrum living.

Look around you. Listen. Everything is buzzing and alive with energy. The traffic on the street, the laughter of children in the playground, the chirping of crickets, the whistle of wind in the trees – all are animated by a potent life-force.

That same energy lives inside you, pulsing through every cell, moving your muscles, activating your mind. You may be a body of some 30 trillion cells, but there is a hidden architecture that holds all these cells together, day after day, year after year, and maintains the coherence that is you. Think of it as the *architecture of your soul*.

Deep within this architecture lie seven precious jewels, spinning in colourful splendour. These jewels are sacred centres of transformation, stepping stones on the journey of healing and awakening. Each one is an energy centre, called a *chakra*, a word that means "wheel" or "disc." Like beads on a necklace, these radiant jewels of energy are strung together along the inner cord of the soul, the vertical core within you that stretches from the base of your spine to the top of your head.

Welcome to the wonderful world of the chakra system: a network of seven major energy centres arranged vertically along the core of your body. In its totality, this map represents a profound formula for wholeness. If you address your life through the lens of each of the areas represented by these seven chakras, you have a template for becoming balanced and whole.

Your chakra architecture can be viewed in different ways, depending on how you travel through it. When examined as a pattern that moves from the ground upwards, it represents a *ladder for liberation*, a way you can systematically free yourself from limiting patterns and move towards greater personal freedom, liberating yourself chakra by chakra.

When viewed from the top down, the seven chakras represent a *map for manifestation*, enabling you to crystallize your ideas into material form through a step-by-step process for creating the life of your dreams.

And for the larger collective of humanity, the chakra system provides a *template for transformation*, a model for the evolution of higher consciousness.

Once you learn this profound system, it can be a guide for the rest of your life. It will help you navigate your relationships, raise your children more consciously, and take action in the world. It will help you traverse the terrain between your mind and body, between spirit and matter, and between heaven and Earth, bringing all these elements into union. Most of all, it will take you to the deepest place within you – what I call the Inner Temple – the place where you'll find the most direct connection with your higher source.

Chakras function best when they are aligned vertically, slightly in front of the spinal column. This allows the vital energy to stream evenly up and down the core of the body, the central pillar of the inner architecture. While the deeper alignment of chakras usually requires a good deal of inner work, the exercise below is a very simple practice you can do anytime to begin the process of bringing your chakras into alignment. It's as simple as sending your roots down while lifting up your crown. When you do this exercise repeatedly, you will become more aware of the core that runs up and down your centre, where all the chakras are arranged in a vertical channel. Finding your core helps you access the energy of each chakra.

Exercise: Roots down, crown up

- Whenever you sit, whether that is sitting in front of your computer, sitting down to eat, getting ready to drive a car, or preparing for meditation, make a point of finding your way to an erect spine. As you take your seat, imagine gently pressing the tip of your tailbone – the part that curls under you like the remnants of a little tail – towards the back of your seat, towards what we call the "back-body."

- As you do this, imagine widening your hips slightly, as if you're making your base wider and grounding it into the Earth, much as the trunk of a tree widens as it meets the ground.

- From this wide seat, press your sitting bones downwards and imagine you have roots coming out of the base of your spine, pushing down into the Earth.

- Take a deep breath and relax as you exhale, letting everything settle gently downwards. Connect with the place you are in – its location, its essence, and the ground beneath you.

- Once you feel sufficiently grounded, raise yourself upwards towards your crown chakra, which is located at the centre of the top of your head. Make sure to keep your roots down even as you lift your crown, stretching your spine in two directions, upwards and downwards.

- Now imagine the seven radiant jewels of your chakras strung along the centre line that runs between your crown and your base. As you move your crown and base away from each other, that centre line becomes straighter and begins to bring your chakras into alignment.

- Inwardly chant the word "I," as if this vertical column were making the capital letter "I" in your deepest core.

- Keep this core vertically aligned between heaven and Earth, even as you read further in this book.

My journey of discovery

I have been blessed to have worked with the chakra system for over 40 years, conducting thousands of healing sessions on a wide variety of people: men and women, old and young, of various nationalities, races, religions, and sexual preferences. My experience inspired me to write a number of bestselling books, which in turn led me to teach workshops and give training courses all over the world, which I've done for the last three decades. And while I have studied with many teachers along the way, it is my students and clients who have taught me the most.

It was 1975 when I first discovered yoga and began reading everything I could find on spirituality and metaphysics. I had majored in psychology as an undergraduate, but the standard theories of the time had left me unsatisfied. I just couldn't accept that the human spirit could be quantified by lab experiments that defined predictable behaviour. I saw each individual as uniquely beautiful, while also challenged by their wounds. I embraced my studies in psychology with vigour, but saw it as more of an art than a science. I kept looking for that ineffable essence that makes us all tick. What theories spoke to our shared commonality yet also embraced our uniqueness?

My studies in spirituality were equally unsatisfying because they failed to address the whole person. I couldn't agree with the idea that we were here to renounce our Earthly existence, as if our daily life didn't matter, and seek some otherworldly state that only a few could achieve. I found as much spirituality in my healing practice, in raising my children, in gardening, in hiking in the wilderness, in creating art, or cooking dinner, as in meditation or on my yoga mat.

I was even sceptical about the first information I heard about the chakra system. I couldn't accept the idea that we needed to repress the lower three chakras because they were evil or negative in order to reach some disembodied state of enlightenment, when all around me I saw disembodied people suffering because of their estrangement from the Earth and their own flesh. I couldn't accept a philosophy that advised denying the body, the reality of this glorious Earth, and the potent life-force that sings through all of creation. Yet I did understand there was a transcendent power that both penetrated and embraced everything. Having been initiated into TM (Transcendental Meditation) at the ripe old age of 21, I had fallen in love with meditation and spent quite a bit of time each day frolicking in that exquisite state of transcendence. There was even a time when I meditated two hours a day and only needed to sleep four hours a night.

I was most fascinated by consciousness itself. What was this capacity to be aware? What could be attained by practices that expanded consciousness, such as yoga and meditation, learning and study? I even experimented with mind-expanding substances and actually found them to be useful as a way of opening a door to the wonders of consciousness, yet they provided only a glimpse of what was possible. To pass through that door required consistent spiritual practice, what yogis called *sadhana*.

As I passionately embraced my own practice, first with TM and then yoga, followed by the gradual purification of my diet and activities, I experienced profound changes in my own consciousness. Colours became brighter, my spirit was lighter, and all that I was doing seemed to be guided by an invisible hand that was shaping my destiny: *to bring the ancient chakra system back to the modern world as a map for guiding humanity on its evolutionary journey to the next stage of civilization.*

That's a mouthful, but I really do see this map as showing the way to both our personal and our collective transformation. It shows us the way back to wholeness, the way through our global rite of passage to the future of civilization, and the way to wake up to the glory of being fully alive.

I have looked at this profound system from just about every angle possible, as both a window to the human soul and a lens through which to view and embrace the outer world. I have seen how it can change people's lives and how at this crucial time on our planet it can guide us through our collective transformation as we enter the shift to the next era of consciousness and values, moving from third chakra to fourth chakra, or from the love of power to the power of love. As we make this transition in our own lives, we help make this shift in our collective organizing principles.[1]

I come to this knowledge through a variety of disciplines – as a somatic psychotherapist, yoga teacher, body worker, historian, and evolutionary philosopher. My lifelong fascination with the healing process and social change, coupled with my proclivity for seeing patterns in both

---

1. For more on this topic, see Anodea Judith, *The Global Heart Awakens: Humanity's Rite of Passage from the Love of Power to the Power of Love,* Shift Books, San Rafael, CA, 2013.

individuals and culture, has honed my work over the last four decades. I have come to recognize the chakra system as a profound ordering system that has the capacity to embrace the full spectrum of human possibility and develop our true potential. This path is not a religion in itself. It can be used with any belief system or religion, for it is a universal model. It contains vital keys to our inner psychology – the unconscious programs that govern how we feel, think, and behave.

My background as both a body-based psychotherapist and yoga teacher allows me to combine the work of inner psychology with both physical practices and spiritual awakening. In fact, I see these aspects of our being as inseparable. We cannot awaken spiritually without healing our psychological wounds, nor can we complete that process of healing without simultaneously awakening. We cannot ignore the role of the body in how we think and feel, nor ignore the role of the mind and emotions in our physical health.

The beauty of the chakra system is that it is all-inclusive. It denies nothing, yet clearly points the way through our difficulties towards freedom.

Where does the chakra system come from?

My first visit to India blew my mind and heart wide open. Every one of my senses was stimulated, if not assaulted, from the moment I stepped off the plane. The scent of exotic spices wafted over the smell of car exhaust and rotting garbage. The bright colours of the women in saris selling flowers and cloth in the marketplace stimulated my visual senses. The noise of incessant traffic punctuated by hucksters selling their wares surrounded me every moment with a background percussion of honking trucks, revving motorbikes, clucking chickens, mooing cows, and barking dogs. Energy flowed in bustling chaos on every street corner, yet somehow hung together in a teeming cacophony of life. Everything around me begged to be touched or felt with an immediacy that impacted every one of my chakras. Here was a land of great beauty and profound spiritual wisdom, paradoxically coupled with horrible filth and bone-chilling poverty.

India is the birthplace of the chakra system, most specifically through the yoga tradition. The exact origins of the system are hard to pinpoint, as it is likely that the philosophy was an oral teaching long before it was written down. The esoteric texts that specifically focus on the chakras were written around the 10th century of the Common Era, during what is known as the Tantric period of yoga philosophy, approximately 500 to 1200CE.

While those in the West tend to think of Tantra as primarily dealing with sexuality, the Tantric doctrines of India wove together many spiritual philosophies, of which sexuality was only a very small part. The essence of Tantric teachings focuses more on the integration of archetypal polarities, such as mind and body, above and below, inside and outside. Especially important is the union between the divine feminine and divine masculine, as seen through the archetypes of the god, Shiva, representing pure consciousness, and the goddess, Shakti, representing the primordial energy from which everything is created. Through the stepping stones of the chakra system, Shiva and Shakti have a way to unite in their eternal love, centred in the heart.

The word "Tantra" also has a meaning similar to a loom – a tool for weaving cloth. When you work with a loom, you stretch a string from one side to the other, back and forth, hooking it each time on opposite sides. Then you take another thread and weave it over and under all the way across and back. This weaving of polarities from one side to the other is what creates a sturdy fabric. According to the Tantric philosophies, weaving together archetypal polarities creates the fabric of reality.

Belief systems that regard the mind as more important than the body, spirit as real and matter an illusion, or men as having the right to be more privileged than women, do not represent a healthy balance of these polarities. If you look at the way the web of life is fraying in today's world, you can see that this imbalance has created health and environmental problems through denial of the body and the Earth, not to mention an inferior status for women and minorities. In the true Tantric tradition, coming to wholeness means bringing these polarities back into balance and unity. This preserves the fabric of reality. The chakra system is the model for doing just that.

A system whose time has come

In the early 1900s Sigmund Freud was one of the first in modern times to address the subtle distinctions in the human psyche by describing the id, the ego, and the superego. At the same time Carl Gustav Jung added a spiritual dimension and revealed the vast realm of the unconscious as he described the light and the shadow, and the inner feminine and masculine, called the *anima* and *animus*. Yet neither theory included the role of the body in our psychological development.

Later, physicians and massage therapists focused on the physical body, but for the most part they failed to address the spiritual dimension. Then yoga became very popular, bringing a spiritual dimension to the body, yet yoga tends to ignore the psychological wounds that lurk beneath the surface.

What is needed is a simple yet elegant system that can embrace the whole person: mind, body, and spirit, or energy. The chakra system speaks to the energetic reality of being human in today's world, as it is mapped onto the physical body yet points to dimensions that are far more than just the body. It reunites the physical and spiritual, putting them on an intersecting continuum of subtle vibration ranging from gross matter to refined consciousness.

Carl Jung said that everyone needed a guiding "archetype of wholeness," which is a model, or "recipe" if you will, for becoming whole. The chakra system is exactly that: a guiding formula for doing what it takes to find and maintain wholeness. But even more, it is a way to achieve greatness, the full potential of who we are.

As I travel around the world with my teachings, I find that people are hungry for a sense of the sacred, which has been separated from everyday life, at least in the West. People have lost touch with their sacred interior, the sacred meaning to life, and why we are here, along with an easy way to talk about it and share that sacred space with others. Navigating the sacred centres of the chakras helps to bring us back home to a place where things become sacred once again.

And finally, as we navigate the difficult changes that are happening globally, through environmental, social, political, and economic imbalances and crises, we need a map to guide us through the chaos into something meaningful yet practical. Even more, we need a vision for what we are becoming as we go through these changes. I believe that our crises are an initiation into a higher state of awareness, a state that is required if we are to survive as a species into the future. The chakras bring us in touch with our divine nature – the eternal within that can keep us steady in times of change.

As portals between the inner and outer worlds, the chakra system gives us a map to heal not only ourselves, but the world we share. As we reclaim and restore the Earth, the waters, the fires, and the air, we are restoring the sacred elements of the chakras. As we bring vision and consciousness to our society and speak truth to our airwaves, we find we have a guideline for creating a thriving and glorious future.

The chakra system provides an archetypal map that is even more pertinent today than it was long ago. Perhaps the ancients knew there would be a time when this wisdom would be needed. I believe that time is now.

So, what's a chakra?

So, let's define what we're talking about when we use the word "chakra." Properly pronounced with a hard "ch," as in "church," *chakra* is a word from Sanskrit (the spiritual language of ancient India), meaning "wheel" or "disc." Chakras are whirling centres of life-force energy occurring in what is called the energy body or subtle body. They are not physical in the literal sense – you couldn't dissect someone on an operating table and find or replace one of their chakras! – yet they are experienced *in* the physical body as a subtle activation of energy in various locations, such as the heart, belly, or throat.

The word "subtle" is very important in learning how to discern this energy, because it is indeed subtle and sometimes difficult to feel. It often requires a refined perception to see and feel beneath the surface to the hidden energy that animates the body's experience. However, at other times a chakra's activation may be quite blatant, such as butterflies in your stomach, a frog in your throat, a flutter in your heart – or even the ecstasy of an orgasm.

Here's a simple exercise to feel the subtle energy in your hands, where you have minor chakras in each palm:

Exercise: Opening the hand chakras

- Extend your arms out in front of you, keeping your elbows straight, with one hand facing up and the other hand facing down.

- Open and close your palms about 20 times rapidly, making sure to open them all the way and close them all the way.

- As your hands begin to tire, move them out a little wider than your shoulders and slowly bring your palms towards each other.

- Pause when your palms are facing each other about 15 centimetres (six inches) apart and see if you can sense a subtle field of energy between your hands. It should feel a bit like the field between two weak magnets, and you might find that your hands tingle slightly.

You just opened the chakras in your hands! How does that feel? These chakras don't have a lot of blockages compared to the central seven chakras, so they are much easier to open. As they open, they emit more energy. At the same time, they become more sensitive to receiving sensations, so the combination makes it easy to have a direct experience of their energy.

Expanding and contracting the hands stimulates this energy in the same way that a massage therapist squeezing and releasing your foot several times would stimulate more feeling in your feet. This expansion and contraction reflects the Tantric nature of the philosophy behind the chakra system.

You can use the same principle of expansion and contraction for the major chakras along the core of the body; however, it's a little more complicated. Yoga stimulates the chakras in precisely that way through various postures called *asanas*. As we talk about each chakra individually in the following chapters, we will explore various exercises for working with each chakra.

Your inner chambers

Chakras are like chambers in the temple of the body. They receive energy, then process it or assimilate it, and later express it. In your home, for example, your kitchen is where you bring in food, cook it and eat it, and then later take out what's left. Your kitchen is actually organized for this task, while your living room is organized for other activities.

In this light, my definition of a chakra is:

> A centre of organization for the reception, assimilation, and expression of life-force energy.

Ideally, each of your chakras can take energy in from the environment, such as food, touch, love, or information, then assimilate that energy, such as digesting the food, or understanding the information, and express it again, such as burning calories exercising, giving love to another, or sharing knowledge. These tasks differ with each chakra.

To accomplish its function, each chakra needs to be developed (you wouldn't want a kitchen with no counters), clean (nor would you want to prepare dinner on dirty work surfaces), and able to perform its functions (you would want your stove and refrigerator to work).

You are a prism

If you think of the primordial energy of the cosmos streaming down into you, then your body is like a prism that breaks that energy down into different colours or frequencies. These different "channels" are correlated to many things, as they map onto the body through seven bundles of nerves branching out from the spinal column, as you can see in the drawing below. Chakras also correspond to glands in the endocrine system, and to physiological systems, such as our respiratory system or digestive system.

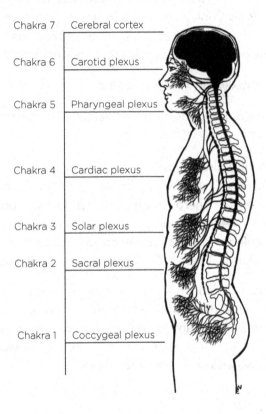

Chakra 7	Cerebral cortex
Chakra 6	Carotid plexus
Chakra 5	Pharyngeal plexus
Chakra 4	Cardiac plexus
Chakra 3	Solar plexus
Chakra 2	Sacral plexus
Chakra 1	Coccygeal plexus

Figure 1: Vertebrae and chakras

Chakras also correspond to archetypal elements, which are named in the ancient texts as earth, water, fire, air, and ether. Ether related to the spiritual world in general and was represented by the upper three chakras, as there were five elements and seven chakras. In my work, I have expanded this to a seven-element system, which is in keeping with the ancient descriptions of each chakra, by replacing ether with sound and adding light and consciousness to correlate with chakras six and seven respectively. In all my decades of working with the chakras, I have found these elements to represent the simplest and most potent way of understanding the differences between each chakra. We will explore this more deeply in the following chapters, but here you can get a quick sense of how they span the full spectrum of our experience:

1. *Earth* is solid. It holds its form and represents the physical world of matter, our foundation, and the Earth, our planet. It correlates to the first chakra at the base of the spine.

2. *Water* is liquid and represents the flow of energy through emotions, sexuality, and movement. It is the element of the second chakra, located in the sacral area.

3. *Fire* is warming and energizing. It is associated with the third chakra and represents the power to take action and the strength of our will.

4. *Air* represents the breath and enters the body through the lungs, to be pumped by the heart to each cell in the body. It is associated with the heart chakra and the energy of love, softness, and expansion.

5. *Sound* is a vibration that can become music, words, and communication. It is related to the fifth centre, known as the throat chakra.

6. *Light* is what enables us to see. It is the element of chakra six, also known as the third eye.

7. *Consciousness* is what allows us to experience all of this: to see and to hear, to love and to act, to feel and to be. It operates through all the chakras, but the mystery of consciousness itself is represented by the crown chakra.

There are many other correspondences as well, and many of these are shown in the chart on pages 20–21. These ideas will be discussed more thoroughly in the chapters on the individual chakras, but for now, just familiarize yourself with the chakra system as a whole, so that you get an idea of how it spans the full spectrum of experience.

How many chakras are there?

This is a question I get asked almost every time I give a lecture or workshop, so it's worth taking a moment to talk about it here. The answer varies, depending on whether you're talking about the seven main chakras, the classic ones, or are including the minor chakras in the hands and feet, or the sub-chakras in the heart, the crown, and the third eye. Some of the ancient texts describe a sub-chakra beneath the heart and mini-chakras in the sixth and seventh chakra, such as the soma chakra or the guru chakra. Some teachers postulate several chakras above and below the body, or minor chakras all over the body.

While I accept that these extra chakras may exist, I find that the seven major chakras form an elegantly profound system without complicating things by adding chakras that are outside the body. I have never met anyone who has mastered all seven of their basic chakras, so this is a good place to start. Working with these chakras will be likely to keep you busy for the rest of your life.

Basically, a chakra is an energy centre, so any place where energy collects could be called a chakra – the stomach, the knees, the elbows, even the fingertips. Here we will be dealing primarily with the seven main chakras and there will be some mention of the chakras of the hands and feet and the Anandakanda Lotus sub-chakra beneath the heart.

Seven identities

We all have an identity. It may be our name, our profession, or our role in life. But did you also know that each chakra gives you an essential part of your identity?

Based on their location in the body, the chakras have come to represent different windows through which we perceive reality. These states of consciousness are all part of our basic identity, and each chakra carries a particular piece of that identity. Each of these identities has a focus for the Self – it is oriented to a basic need or function. We can become overly focused on these identities, or we may give them too little attention and be lacking in these areas.

- *First chakra: Physical identity, oriented to self-preservation.* Here our consciousness focuses on survival issues, such as concerns with safety and security, struggles with money or health, or living in a state of fight or flight. Appropriate identification with our physical body helps keep us alive by attending to our body's needs.

Chakra	Location	Central issue	Goals	Rights	Developmental stage
7	Top of head, cerebral cortex	Awareness	Wisdom, knowledge, consciousness, spiritual connection	To know	Throughout life
6	Centre of head, at brow level	Intuition, imagination	Intuition, imagination, vision	To see	Adolescence
5	Throat	Communication	Clear communication, creativity, resonance	To speak and be heard	7–12 years
4	Heart	Love, relationships	Balance, compassion, self-acceptance, good relationships	To love and be loved	3½–7 years
3	Solar plexus	Power, will	Vitality, spontaneity, strength of will, purpose, self-esteem	To act	18 months–3½ years
2	Abdomen, genitals, lower back, hips	Sexuality, emotions	Fluidity, pleasure, healthy sexuality, feeling, function	To feel, to want	6 months–2 years
1	Base of spine, coccygeal plexus	Survival	Stability, grounding, physical health, prosperity, trust	To be here, to have	Womb–12 months

Identity	Demon	Excessive characteristics	Deficient characteristics	Element	Chakra
Universal identity (self-knowledge)	Attach-ment	Overly intel-lectual, spiritual addiction, confusion, dissociation	Learning difficulties, spiri-tual scepticism, limited beliefs, materialism, apathy	Thought	7
Archetypal identity (self-reflection)	Illusion	Headaches, nightmares, hallucinations, delusions, difficulty concentrating	Poor memory, poor vision, cannot see patterns, denial	Light	6
Creative identity (self-expression)	Lies	Excessive talking, inability to listen, stuttering	Fear of speaking, poor rhythm, aphasia (shyness)	Sound	5
Social identity (self-acceptance)	Grief	Co-dependent, poor boundaries, possessive, jealous, narcissistic	Shy, lonely, isolated, lack of empathy, bitter, critical	Air	4
Ego identity (self-definition)	Shame	Dominating, blaming, aggres-sive, scattered, constantly active	Weak will, poor self-esteem, passive, sluggish, fearful	Fire	3
Emotional identity (self-gratifi-cation)	Guilt	Overly emotional, poor boundaries, sex addiction, indulgent	Rigidity, emotional numbness, fear of pleasure	Water	2
Physical identity (self-pres-ervation)	Fear	Heaviness, slug-gish, monotony, obesity, hoarding, materialism	Frequent fear, lack of discipline, restless, under-weight, spacey	Earth	1

Table showing chakra correspondences

- *Second chakra: Emotional identity, oriented to self-gratification.* This level focuses on how we feel – our desires, urges, and sensations. It's how we sort out what we want and need. This identity asks the questions: "Am I feeling OK, and if not, how can I feel better?"

- *Third chakra: Ego identity, oriented to self-definition.* This is the state of consciousness that focuses on what we are trying to be in the world, how we define ourselves (both to ourselves and others) and what we are trying to accomplish through our actions. Think of it as the executive identity that decides what the "game plan" will be.

- *Fourth chakra: Social identity, oriented to self-acceptance.* The social identity just wants to be loved and accepted by others. It represents our *relational* consciousness, which includes awareness of others and the web of relationships around us. It may create an outer persona at the cost of the true self in order to be accepted. Here we might create a persona that is friendly, helpful, or powerful in order to get people to like us.

- *Fifth chakra: Creative identity, oriented to self-expression.* This level of consciousness is oriented to the realm of communication, including both listening and speaking, as well as creative self-expression. Here we might have an identity as an artist, a musician, a teacher, or a healer.

- *Sixth chakra: Archetypal identity, oriented to self-reflection.* As we grow in awareness, we become aware of the "bigger picture" – larger archetypal patterns that reveal who we are in the greater scheme of things, perhaps our destiny or purpose. It is here we develop our intuition and create a vision for our life.

- *Seventh chakra: Universal identity, oriented to self-knowledge.* As we come into the realm of consciousness itself, we recognize we are part of a universal oneness, and experience unity within and without. This awareness is the true source of self-knowledge.

Currents of energy

The chakras are not only energy *centres* in and of themselves, but are fed by vital currents of subtle energy. These channels are like the highways that bring energy from the divine source into our body. Think of a road map that describes how goods get delivered from the manufacturer to the stores. In yoga philosophy, these highways are called *nadis*, meaning "currents of motion." There are thousands of nadis, ranging from major currents to minor currents, much like our highways range from six-lane freeways to curvy two-lane roads, little back roads, and driveways. Some nadis carry more energy than others.

The three major nadis that energize the chakras are called the *Sushumna*, the *Ida*, and the *Pingala*. The Sushumna nadi is the vertical channel that runs straight up and down our core. In the esoteric texts, it has several layers, with only the centremost layer moving all the way to the crown chakra. Energy can both rise and fall in this central channel, but generally it is seen as rising from the lower chakras to the higher chakras.

The two nadis forming a figure eight-like pattern around the chakras are called *Ida*, meaning "moon," and *Pingala*, meaning "sun." These carry the feminine and masculine energies (respectively) that intertwine like spirals of DNA around the Sushumna. If we posit that they are moving in opposite directions, one flowing up and the other down, then you can see how they stimulate the spinning of the chakras, which move like gears, alternating between clockwise and counterclockwise rotation. As we noted earlier, the chakras act as major gears that take us on the journey through life (see *Figures 2 and 3 opposite*).

Many practitioners and chakra healers believe that the chakras spin only one way, usually clockwise from the perspective of the healer, but I do not believe this makes sense in light of the Tantric nature of the chakra model, which is based on polarities. It is possible to hold a pendulum over the part of the body where a particular chakra is located and notice whether the energy moves the pendulum. Reports vary as to which direction it moves in; however, I do not agree that a chakra is "moving backwards" if the pendulum spins counterclockwise – which is actually clockwise from the perspective of the person's chakra!

Currents of liberation and manifestation

Do you ever feel stuck? Trapped in repeating patterns like habits, addictions, or limiting beliefs? You may want to get out of these patterns, but try as you might, they still persist. Or maybe you're a person who lives in your head. You have lots of great ideas, but don't know how to bring them into manifestation. This is all reflected in how the "liberating" and "manifesting" currents become blocked in their upward and downward flow through the chakras.

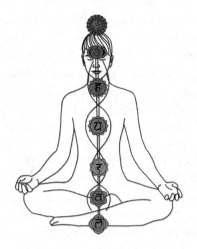

Figure 2: Ida, Pingala *and* Sushumna *nadis*

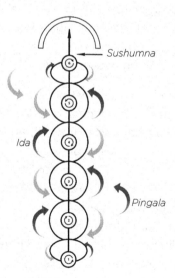

Figure 3: The spinning of the chakras as a result of polaric currents, Ida *and* Pingala

The *current of liberation* flows from the Earth below our feet into the first chakra at the base of our spine and then moves upwards, chakra by chakra, until it pierces the crown and moves beyond it into universal consciousness. In the ancient texts, this rising current was called *mukti*, which means "freedom." Its movement frees us from fixed forms and reaches towards liberation and transcendence.

The descending current begins in the universal heavenly realm. It enters the crown chakra as awareness or thought, and then descends, chakra by chakra, gaining *density* at each step until it manifests on the physical plane. I call this the *manifesting current*, the means through which we bring our dreams into reality. I discuss this current in depth in my book, co-authored with Lion Goodman, called *Creating on Purpose: Manifesting through the Chakras*. In the ancient texts, this downward current was called *bhukti*, which means "enjoyment." It is through the manifestation of the Divine right here on Earth that we enjoy its many forms of expression and bring heaven down to Earth.

The liberating and manifesting currents are constantly mixing energies at each chakra level. At chakra one, the base chakra, we have very little liberation and complete manifestation. This gives us physical form. Once something is set in its form, such as the structure of a house, it is very hard to change, so there is very little liberation at this level. At the crown chakra, however, we have very little manifestation but ultimate liberation. We are free to think or imagine anything with our consciousness, and others cannot see or touch our thoughts as they can our physical form. In the throat chakra, we can hear the manifestation of physical sound, but we cannot see or touch it. At the level of the heart chakra, these currents are perfectly balanced.

We need to have both currents flowing to be full and productive human beings. If we cannot liberate, we get stuck in fixed patterns, and this can create addictions, compulsions, repetitive behaviours, and situations that persist. If we cannot manifest, we cannot move things down from our imagination into tangible reality. We may have difficulty grounding ourselves, feeling our emotions, taking action, or making a living.

The liberating and manifesting currents are the prime connection between heaven and Earth. They move at the same time and animate the spinning of the chakras. They are our most direct access to our source, whether we consider that an inner source or an external, divine source.

Currents of reception and expression

There are two other currents, which are more interpersonal. They run horizontally, making connections between people. These currents are stronger in the middle chakras, where the bulk of our interpersonal exchanges take place.

The *current of reception* takes energy from our environment into the chakras in various ways, such as receiving love, listening to a communication, or seeing a beautiful smile. In turn, we express energy through each of our chakras, perhaps in the form of love, emotion, or ideas, through the *current of expression*.

If either of these currents becomes blocked, then we lose the ability to fully receive or express energy through one or more chakras. We might find it hard to listen or to express ourselves verbally, for example. We might be blocked in our ability to give love or receive love.

Also, when the currents of expression or reception are blocked, the energies inside and around us have more difficulty balancing. As a result we can become *overcharged*, meaning there is too much energy inside that can't get out, or *undercharged* or depleted, meaning that we give energy away without taking it in. Someone who has a challenging job and no time to release their stress will have a lot of unreleased energy and can become overcharged. Someone who is in a job where they are giving all day, such as a nurse or a therapist, will become depleted and undercharged if they don't find a way to take energy in and replenish themselves.

Excess and deficiency

Very few of us really live in balance. Most of us do too much of some things and not enough of others. We are overdeveloped in some chakras and underdeveloped in others. All this results in chakras that become *excessive* or *deficient*, or sometimes a combination of both. Excessive chakras hold too much energy, while deficient chakras have too little. Deficient chakras result from a strategy of *avoidance* and excessive patterns from *over-compensation*. It is important to realize that this is the result of our defence patterns being repeated over time, rather than an original wound, such as not getting enough love or getting too much negative attention.

One of my clients we'll call Sammy avoided feeling his emotions (chakra two) and also taking risks (chakra three).

As a result, when he came to me he couldn't really feel himself in his hips and belly. His second and third chakras had become deficient. Due to this shutdown, his energy was diverted elsewhere – you guessed it – up into his head. He was very smart, but his downward, manifesting current didn't make it all the way to the ground: it got stuck in his deficient chakras. So, even though he was intellectually brilliant, Sammy had trouble manifesting. He was overlooked in his job and had trouble finishing projects.

Marilyn, on the other hand, had a wound in her heart chakra from not getting enough love and recognition as a child. She tried to compensate by being the centre of attention and constantly engaging in social activities. In fact she was unable to be alone. She had developed an excessive heart chakra, which wasn't a case of too much love but of too much focus on trying to get love. As a result, she was so focused on her social life that she had little time for herself and for the quieter, more contemplative realms of the upper chakras. She was fairly grounded, but she couldn't sit still and meditate and had a hard time hearing her own inner voice. Her liberating current was blocked.

If we focus too much on a certain area as compensation for something we are missing, then we create an excessive chakra. If we are compensating for the feeling of weakness by dominating others, our third chakra becomes excessive. If we talk too much, our fifth chakra becomes excessive. Over time these imbalances can become real blockages that impede the free flow of energy through the system. A block in one chakra may impact another chakra, such as living in our head when our connection to our body is deficient, or choosing power at the cost of love.

Balancing the chakras requires balancing excess and deficiency. Chakras that are excessive need to *release energy* in order to come into balance. If we are excessive in our fifth chakra (communication), for example, we need to let go of needing to talk so much. If we are excessive in our first chakra and tend to put on weight as a result (one of the common characteristics of root-chakra excess), then we need to let go of that weight by discharging it as energy through activity. If our third chakra is excessive (power and will), then we need to let go of control.

Chakras that are deficient, in contrast, need to *draw energy inwards*, rather than avoid it. If we avoid connection with our body (first-chakra deficiency), we can focus on the body by getting a massage, working out, or practising yoga. If our power chakra is deficient, we need to stretch ourselves by taking on challenges and risks. If our heart chakra is deficient, we may need to allow ourselves to receive more from others through the current of reception.

How to work with your chakras

> *Spiritual practice is only what you are doing now. Anything else is a fantasy.*
> JACK KORNFIELD

One of the beauties of the chakra system is that it is so multi-dimensional. There are many different ways to access your chakras and to do the work necessary to bring them into balance. It all begins with awareness. What areas of your body are tight or problematic? What parts of your life just don't seem to work very well, such as relationships, health, or making a living? What do you tend to focus on when you're doing something automatic like driving or washing dishes? Do you focus on how you are feeling? That means your second chakra is grabbing your attention. Do you focus on internal conversations with others? That implies your fifth chakra of communication. Do you focus on where your next meal is coming from? That relates to your first chakra of survival. Do you focus on your relationships? This indicates the heart chakra.

Below is a list of various ways you can work with your chakras. Each of the following chapters will include specific exercises that can become part of your chakra toolkit for awakening, healing, and balancing your chakras.

1. *The body.* Physical exercise stimulates the body. Working out gets your energy moving, and when your energy is moving, you can access any of the chakras better. Yoga is designed to stimulate the chakras, and different poses tend to drive energy to different parts of the body, for example hip openers are good for the second chakra, while chest openers are good for the heart chakra. In addition, receiving physical work such as massage or a chiropractic adjustment, or changing your diet will influence your chakras.

2. *Visualization.* You can visualize colour in your various chakras, imagine light moving up and down your core, or channels of energy moving inwards or outwards, or visualize a chakra opening or closing down. The ancient practices involved mostly the visualization of deities and symbols for the chakras.

3. *Chanting.* Each chakra is associated with a seed sound, called a *bija mantra*, which is said to stimulate that

chakra when chanted aloud or intoned silently. (This will be discussed more fully in the chapter on the fifth chakra.)

4. *Breathing practices*, also called *pranayama*. You can focus your breath upon any of the chakras, imagining that the chakra itself is breathing in and out.

5. *Relationship.* When you interact with another person, you interact through all of your chakras. There's nothing like a relationship for bringing up unresolved issues, which may relate to any of the chakras. So a relationship is a wonderful crucible for exploring your chakras.

6. *Outer life.* Your inner work is nothing if it doesn't show up in your outer life. Similarly, there are things you can do outwardly to help develop a chakra, such as organizing your cupboards and material goods (chakra one), writing a poem or learning to sing (chakra five), or taking on a task to develop your will (third chakra), such as a diet or exercise routine.

7. *Energetic healing.* Many practitioners are skilled at removing stagnant energy in the chakras through their hands. Often the hands do not even need to touch the body to create some sense of relief, such as a lightness of being. As energy centres, chakras can be influenced by skilled energy work.

8. *Meditation.* Last, but certainly not least, sitting quietly in meditation allows all your chakras to empty out their old patterns and be renewed with fresh energy. Meditation on a particular chakra can increase awareness at that level. Meditation on a concept connected to a particular

chakra, such as relationships or creativity, can increase awareness of these aspects of your life. Meditation in general is a tonic for the whole body–mind system.

POINTS TO REMEMBER

- Chakras are centres of organization for the reception, assimilation, and transmission of life-force energy.

- The classic system has seven major chakras, with minor chakras in the hands and feet, under the heart, and within the upper chakras.

- Chakras correspond to archetypal elements: earth, water, fire, air, sound, light, and consciousness.

- Chakras are the focal points of vital currents of energy within the body. The four main currents are the currents of liberation and manifestation, reception and expression.

- Chakras can become excessive or deficient. Excessive chakras are the result of compensating strategies, while deficient chakras are the result of avoidance.

Chakra One

EARTH

Chakra One

Earth

*We won't have peace on the earth, until
we make peace with the earth.*
JULIA BUTTERFLY HILL

Location:	Base of the spine
Name and meaning:	Muladhara, root support
Purposes:	Embodiment, grounding, engagement
Element:	Earth
Principle:	Gravity
Developmental age:	Womb through first year
Identity:	Physical identity
Orientation:	Self-preservation
Demon:	Fear
Right:	To have
Seed sound:	*Lam*
Colour:	Red
Balanced form:	Grounded, solid, stable

Getting down to Earth

If you're going to get down to basics, you have to get down to earth, down to the root of things. Here's where you find the foundation of the chakra system, and here's where you begin your long journey up the spine. The root chakra, located at the base of the spine, governs the lower part of the torso, including the legs and feet, the large intestine and colon, and the bones in general, as the hardest parts of the body. If you have issues in any of these tissues, regard them as an invitation to open and balance your first chakra.

Building a solid foundation supports everything else you do, which reflects the Sanskrit name of this chakra, *Muladhara*, meaning "root support," also translated as "foundation." A fitting name, as your roots dig into the first-chakra element of *earth* and give you the foundation, support, and nourishment that are necessary for survival – the very first challenge in the game of life. This level of consciousness is oriented to *self-preservation*, especially through your ability to identify with your physical body and its basic needs – in order not only to stay alive but to thrive.

Just as a flower pot holds the dirt firmly around the roots of the plant to create stability, the structural aspects of your life – your home, job, physical body, diet, and exercise – hold you and give you the support to live a long and healthy life. If you are the kind of person who resists structure or avoids paying attention to this level of existence, you are missing the benefits of a strong first chakra, which provides support for everything that follows.

Many people interpret the spiritual path as moving away from the element earth, as this element is dense, heavy, and limited. Indeed, focusing on this level is often viewed as "materialistic," the very antithesis to spirituality. In my 40 years of working with the chakra system, however, I have found that nothing could be further from the truth. Grounding is an essential part of spiritual development. Any gardener will tell you that a plant needs deep roots to grow tall. If you tried to help your flowers reach the heavens faster by pulling them up by their roots, what would happen? In contrast, the better the soil, and the deeper and stronger the roots, the better a plant can withstand the sun, wind, and rain, and the higher it can grow towards the heavens. Rather than being a negation of spirituality, the roots of the first chakra are where the spiritual journey begins!

The first chakra's paradox

This points out the basic principle of the first chakra, which is a paradox: *you must push down in order to rise up.* Think of what happens when you jump. You first bend your knees, then push against the ground. The deeper you bend and the harder you push, the higher you jump. It's also true that the firmer the ground, the easier it is to jump. It's much more difficult to jump on a sandy beach, for example, than on concrete. So, having a solid foundation gives you something firm to push down into and allows you to remain safe and stable while rising up to higher consciousness and the upper chakras. This solidity is a kind of containment that allows the energy within you to build and rise up.

Pushing against the solid plane of the Earth is also a kind of energetic engagement. Like a clutch engaging with the gears in an automobile, engagement with the Earth plane *energizes the body and gets things moving.*

If the first chakra is off-balance or your base foundation is not solid, you will develop compensations or avoidance in most of the other chakras. Sandra, for example, doesn't feel truly grounded, and compensates with her third chakra, oriented to power, by controlling everything around her. George compensates for being disconnected from his body by living in his head and trying to figure everything out in order to feel safe.

Consequently, problems in any of the chakras could have their "roots" in the base chakra. My friend Amy, for example, complains about feeling powerless in her life, when the source of that weakness is actually shaky ground. Getting to the root of things is always a good place to start with any issue.

When the Muladhara chakra is open and balanced, you'll feel stable in your life, healthy in your body, solid in who you are, and grounded in your daily activities. You'll be able to manifest easily and live in abundance and right livelihood. But getting this chakra balanced is no easy task!

Understanding the first-chakra symbol

The four petals shown in the symbol of the first chakra can be seen as representing the four directions, north, east, south, and west, that provide our orientation in physical space.

The square inside the circle represents the solidity that comes with a base that nestles firmly into the ground. Think of "getting back to square one" or "squaring things up" to make them solid.

The Sanskrit letter inside the square is the *bija mantra*, or seed sound, which is pronounced *Lam*. Repeating this sound is said to activate the element earth.

The animal is an elephant with seven trunks, a heavy animal who is grounded and earthy, but with a trunk that can connect with each of the six other chakras.

Within the solidity of the square is a downward-pointing triangle, representing the feminine "Shakti-power," which is energized by pushing downwards yet expands as it moves upwards. Within that triangle is the Shiva lingam, the male principle, which rises upwards, held by the feminine Shakti. Wrapped three-and-a-half times around it is the divine serpent energy, known as Kundalini. As the first chakra becomes energized, Kundalini is said to unwind and begin her journey up the spine, piercing and awakening each chakra in turn.

The Kundalini process can be smooth and graceful, or it can be a very bumpy ride that shakes up everything in your life. If you are properly grounded and your chakras are open and ready to take on the additional current of the Kundalini energy, this awakening can be blissful. If the ground is solid, the upward journey is more coherent. If the ground is shaky, the journey becomes chaotic.

It's all in the instincts

Good instincts usually tell you what to do before your head has figured it out.
Michael Burke

My client Emily had always ignored her body. A single mother, she worked herself to the bone, trying to be the ideal university professor and perfect mother at the same time. All of this came to a sudden halt when she was diagnosed with breast cancer. Understandably, this threat to her survival dominated her consciousness. She did survive, but not without a radical change in her priorities, eating habits, exercise routines, and attitudes. She had to return to her body's basic instincts and learn how to listen to their wisdom. It was back to basics and the first chakra.

The challenge of survival is the very first challenge we face on our journey. We've got to stay in the game in order to play. Fortunately, our bodies are hard-wired to survive, equipped with instincts that make us sweat when we're hot and shiver when we're cold, jump at a loud noise, or prepare to run from danger, all without having to think about it. Beneath the radar of awareness, our heart beats out its rhythm, our lungs expand and contract, and our stomach harvests the vitamins and calories of each bite.

This body-based intelligence is largely *instinctual* – hard-wired into the nervous system, the way a computer is hard-wired when we bring it home from the store. Our instincts come from an ancient and primitive part of the brain, which literally takes over our consciousness whenever we feel threatened. If someone points a gun at us or if we are suddenly evicted from our home or lose our job, then it will be difficult to think of anything else until these threats to our survival and security are resolved. Once resolution takes place, then our attention is freed up to frolic at higher levels of consciousness.

Therefore, our survival consciousness is primary, which is why it's the very first chakra. It will regulate our thoughts and actions, the movement of our blood and muscles, and all our available energy when necessary to keep our body alive and safe. Our species wouldn't have evolved as far as it has without this primary mechanism. We have the ability to override these instincts, but we do so at our own peril, for it can make us sick, disembodied, and out of touch with ourselves and the reality around us.

Grounding the body

> There is more wisdom in your body than in your deepest philosophy.
> FRIEDRICH NIETZSCHE

Survival consciousness connects us to our *physical identity*, whose orientation is *self-preservation*. This means we can identify with the needs of our body. If we are balanced in this identity, we know when we're hungry or tired, when we need to stretch or move or be still, and where our body is in physical space.

If we are *under-identified* with our body, we don't notice these things. We might get overtired, forget to eat, or clumsily bump into things. If we are *over-identified*, however, we can become preoccupied with the body, and indeed trapped in its endless demands, obsessively worrying about every ache or twitch, or fretting about an extra kilo. Physical identity is important for survival, but ideally, when we feel safe and secure, it should move into the background of consciousness, and allow us to think about other things.

Our body is the vehicle we've been given to take the journey through life. We only get one per lifetime, so it is important to care for it well. It's the only thing we know we will have for the rest of our life. Far from being a place where we are trapped in physicality, it is a most exquisite vehicle – one that can take us anywhere we want to go with full sensory involvement. The mind may rationalize and believe things that aren't true, but the body never lies. It contains a grain of truth that is undeniable.

While all the chakras have a location in the body, the first chakra relates to the task of *embodiment*. Our health, our fitness, and our ability to listen to our body have a direct bearing on other aspects of the first chakra: our ability to be stable and prosperous, to be present, to set boundaries – in short, to have enough and to know when we have enough.

Exercise: Basic grounding

Your two legs are like the two prongs of a plug that plug into the circuit of the Earth. Once you are plugged in, you can receive the different frequencies of each chakra. But first you need to energize your legs to carry this energy between the Earth and the body.

Step one

• Stand upright with your feet shoulder-width apart. Place your feet so that your heels are slightly farther apart than your toes, so that you are a bit pigeon-toed. Make sure that you aren't locking your knees by bending them just slightly and extending them towards the second toe of each foot. *This is your basic grounding stance.*

• Now energize that stance by pressing your feet *down and out* on the floor, as if you were trying to push apart the floorboards between your feet. Notice how it makes your body feel more solidly planted in the Earth and how you feel more present.

Practising this stance will serve you when you need to be grounded in the face of adversity.

Step two

Now that you have the basic stance, you can energize your legs to bring more energy up from the Earth to activate your first chakra. As your first chakra becomes activated, the energy may eventually spill over and rise to the other chakras. Learning to do this is a good way to ground the higher chakras into the body's stability.

• Standing as above, with your feet pressing down and out, inhale and bend your knees, imagining that you are drawing Earth energy upwards through your legs and into your first chakra.

- As you exhale, slowly push *through the core* of each leg, pressing down and out with your feet as if you were pushing the floor away, and begin to straighten your legs. Be careful not to lock your knees: straighten your legs only about 90 per cent of the way, keeping a slight bend at the knee. Locking the knees will shut off the charge you are trying to build up in your legs.

- Repeat this movement for a minute or two, moving very slowly between bending your knees as you inhale and pushing through your legs and slightly straightening as you exhale. Make sure the movement is slow and not mechanical and that you are *engaging* with the solidity of the Earth plane as a way of pushing energy through your legs.

- In most cases, you will begin to feel a slight trembling in your legs after a few minutes of doing this exercise. Know that the trembling is exactly the effect you are trying to achieve. It represents new energy coming into the roots of your legs. See if you can allow that trembling to move through your legs without stopping it. In fact, find out just what increases it, and do more of that. Does it increase when your legs are almost straight and you are pushing the floor away? Does it increase as you bend your knees or as you press the floorboards apart? You will notice that the longer you do this exercise, the more pronounced the trembling becomes. That's exactly what's supposed to happen.

- Continue to build the charge in your legs and see if you can allow it into your body. If at any point you feel uncomfortable with the trembling, as if it is giving you too much energy, simply stop the exercise and kick out your legs or stamp your feet. That will discharge some of the energy and bring you back to normal.

How and why to use this exercise

- when you feel sluggish or sleepy

- when you need to be more grounded and focused

- to feel more embodied

- to strengthen your legs

- to find stability

- to bring more energy into your body

Ways to enhance this exercise

- Say the word "I" as you push into the ground.

- Visualize the "I" as the vertical core of energy within you.

- Continue with the words "I am" and see that vertical "I" as expanding to the edge of your body.

- Add the words "I am in here" to feel that you are fully occupying your body.

- Finish with "I am in here and this is mine" as a way of owning your ground.

Things to avoid

- Avoid getting overly energized if you are subject to anxiety.

- Avoid shallow breathing that can make you feel dizzy. If you do feel dizzy, bend forwards at the waist and let your head hang lower than your hips.

- Avoid straightening your knees all the way.

- Avoid anything that brings pain into your body, especially if you have prior injuries to the knees, ankles, or feet.

Developmental stage of the first chakra

Ideally, embodiment occurs during the first year of life, as we move from the womb to the world. Being touched and held by our parents directs the mind–body interface to tune in to bodily sensations, just as when we get a foot massage, we suddenly remember our feet again. Our parents are our first link with the physical world, and they act as both connection and protection. As connectors, they bring warmth and holding, food and comfort, connecting us to what we need in order to survive. They take care of us when we're too young to take care of ourselves, and that gives us a feeling of safety and security. Our mother, in particular, figures strongly during our first year of life, when our consciousness is largely centred on getting the basic functions of the body working, such as eating, digesting, grasping, crawling, and walking.

If you were not held and touched while you were "finding" your body, then you literally have to hold yourself energetically. That may feel like a matter of life and death, where your very survival depends on being able to hold yourself together. This results in an energetic holding pattern around the first chakra, one that can't let go enough to trust the outer world and receive what it has to offer. Without that trust, you may question your basic "right to have," and find difficulty in manifesting money, jobs, home, or relationships. Or, like some clients I have worked with, you could initially have these things, but not be able to hold on to them. You might make a fortune then lose it, or change jobs too frequently to gain seniority or traction in any of them.

In order to "have" what you need and want in life, you must be able to expand the first chakra's natural tendency to hold on, so that there is room to receive. The grounding exercise above can help with that, but so can the following affirmations:

- I am safe.
- I have what I need to survive.
- I can take care of myself.
- I love my body.
- I am supported.
- I have a right to be here.
- I am solid.
- I am *in* here.
- This body is mine.

The bulk of our first-chakra "program" is written into our psyche and nervous system during the first year of life. From birth to first steps, we are busy growing a body and figuring out how to be in the physical world. At this infant state, survival needs must be supplied by others, as we are too helpless to supply them for ourselves. If these needs are properly attended to, we get the message, deep in our primitive brain, that the world is a safe place, and we will have what we need in order to survive. In other words, we will develop a solid sense of ground. If this doesn't happen, then the first chakra may be compromised or traumatized, depending on the severity of the situation, and the rest of our life built on a shaky foundation.

You may be one of the many people who did not feel safe and secure growing up. Neglect, abandonment, violence, poverty, and illness are all issues that negatively impact the first chakra's ability to be grounded and create safety, security, and abundance in later life. In fact, these issues, if left unresolved, will continue to hijack the energy from other chakras, and keep you in a kind of highly charged survival consciousness, even when it is unwarranted. This might lead to hyper-vigilance towards everything around you, difficulty relaxing or sleeping, or overreaction when someone speaks to you. Then you need to practise some grounding to help the body feel safer and more secure, and learn to hold yourself lovingly and compassionately, the way a child would want to be held.

Facing your fear

I learned that courage was not the absence of fear, but the triumph over it.
Nelson Mandela

Lack of safety creates the "demon" of the first chakra, which is fear. Fear is only a demon when it's a carry-over from the past that keeps us overly guarded in the present. It is entirely appropriate if our survival is threatened in some way, such as being in a truly dangerous situation – a car out of control or a situation of violence, for example.

The body's reaction to fear is to heighten its own energy or "charge" with a readiness to do whatever it takes to protect itself. We generally call this a "fight or flight" reaction. The body is flooded with stress hormones, especially from the adrenal glands, to enable it to take action. But what often happens, especially to children, is that the fear arises, along with the increased charge in the body, but the fight or flight cannot take place. There is either nowhere to run or the person is too little or too scared to fight.

When this happens, the charge in the first chakra isn't released into action and instead becomes trapped in a "frozen" state. It cannot be accessed, and this creates a first-chakra block. It may be that our legs become frozen and we can no longer feel our ground. It may be that our instincts become frozen and our physical identity is distorted – we may think we need more or less food or sleep, for example, than we actually do. This constant state of underlying fear can be exhausting, especially for the adrenal glands, and can lead to adrenal exhaustion.

We transform our demons by facing them squarely. Owning our fear by claiming the charge that runs through the body is a way to transform it into an ally. This means that we notice when there is an increase of charge in our body and instead of interpreting it as fear, reframe it as the potency of our basic vitality.

Allow that charge to enter and enliven your tissues, and you will feel more embodied. Use that energy to do something constructive, like clean your house or go for a walk, and you will then be "harvesting" that charge instead of perpetuating a cycle of fear that gets further frozen into the tissue.

Excess and deficiency in the first chakra

Two women stood before me as first-chakra volunteers in one of my workshops. Both had abandonment issues from childhood. One had been adopted at birth, the other had "lost" her mother to alcohol and never received the nurturing and support she needed. But these two women were as different as night and day. The adopted child had created a large, solid body and had struggled all her life with weight issues. The child of the alcoholic was tall and skinny, with bright eyes and a big smile, but was disconnected from her body and the Earth. They both had mother wounds that produced fear in their bodies, but their methods of dealing with their wounds were vastly different.

The heavier woman had an *excessive* first-chakra strategy: increasing her body's weight to feel more grounded and substantial. The original separation from her birth mother had produced a fear that had remained deep in her tissues, even though her adult mind knew she was safe. Her excess weight was her compensation for the underlying feeling that she was unwanted and her life didn't matter. It was as if she had to make a large body to avoid disappearing or being overlooked. While this made sense from an instinctual survival level of consciousness, it was not serving her health or vitality to carry so much weight, and it was now an obstacle in her life. Excess weight is often an indication of an excessive coping strategy in the first chakra, though other chakras can sometimes be implicated as well.

The thinner woman lived in her head. It was clear she was very smart, and she wanted to understand the exercise thoroughly before she attempted it. Intellectually, she knew "why" she felt insubstantial, but she had long since flown out of her body and was having trouble getting back in. She had issues with self-nourishment and trust, and tended to be fearful and hyper-vigilant of everything around her. Moving upwards in her chakras, away from her ground, was an avoidance strategy that created a deficient first chakra. She couldn't gain weight if she tried, but she would lose weight whenever she was under stress.

Notice that both women had a similar first-chakra wound: *abandonment.* Neither had got quite what she needed to properly ground her precious being in the world and come into full embodiment in her life. This demonstrates how the same wound can lead to excessive behaviour in one person and deficient behaviour in another. This stems from whatever strategies worked best when we were growing up. The trouble comes when we keep those strategies as we grow older. What worked when we were young is often an obstacle later on.

Different as they were, for both women the healing was similar. The gates of the first chakra needed to be opened and grounded. Once the "gates" of a chakra are open, the energy tends to self-regulate, just as hot and cold start to equalize when we open a door to the outside world on a warm or cold day.

I took both women into the exercise of physical grounding described above. This exercise is designed to engage with the Earth plane through the legs and feet in a way that brings energy, or charge, into the first chakra consciously and deliberately. Practising it over time creates a feeling of safety and solidity in our being, so that the body no longer has to compensate or avoid. Of course this doesn't happen instantly – these exercises are cumulative and depend on creating new habits. They establish patterns slowly, through retraining the energy body to "hold" the energy in the tissue appropriately: neither too much nor too little.

Below you will see a list of excessive and deficient first-chakra qualities. Some people fall clearly on one side or the other, while others show characteristics in both directions. These are the many ways that we try to find balance through avoiding or compensating in different areas of the same chakra.

Excessive and deficient qualities in the first chakra

Excessive qualities	Deficient qualities	Balanced qualities
Overweight	Underweight	Physically healthy
Stubborn, resistant to change	Fearful, anxious	Stable
Heavy, sluggish	Restless	Grounded
Overly bound to structure	Resists structure	Solid
Materialistic, greedy	Prone to poverty consciousness	Prosperous, has right livelihood
Trapped in the body	Disconnected from the body	Present in the body

The role of structure

As a freedom-lover by nature, it has taken me a long time to appreciate the first chakra's role of structure. In my younger days, I resisted any kind of structure that was put upon me. Even if I had no choice, such as being in school and having the structure of classes, I would resent it and inwardly rebel against it. It felt constricting, as if it would limit me.

Years later, when I was living in an alternative community, with a lifestyle about as free as you can get, I realized that neither I nor any of my friends was really getting anywhere in life. I asked that age-old question, "If we're so smart, why aren't we rich?" Talent and intelligence were abundant, but tangible results were weak. What we all had in common was that we resisted structure.

I then began to see structure as *support*, something that actually *brought* freedom rather than constricted it. After that realization, I was able to go back into education, get my higher degrees, accept jobs that required commitments, enter lasting relationships, and raise kids to adulthood. My life began to gain traction, and with a more solid ground beneath me, I was able to achieve my dreams.

Structures are necessary for accomplishing anything that is difficult: building a business, getting in shape, writing a book, maintaining a relationship, or earning a living. Structures such as the 12-step programme of Alcoholics Anonymous (and all its offshoots) help addicts not only become sober but also maintain their sobriety. Programmes of learning are structured to support the students' progress, for example classes that build on one another. We may need a grounding in certain subjects to take our knowledge to a higher level.

Our bones create structure for our body, and if we didn't have them we couldn't stand up. Spiritual practices, such as yoga, meditation, diet or exercise, are structures that support the expansion of our consciousness. Though they may seem constricting, ultimately structures do bring freedom, just as dirt holding the roots of a plant allows it to flower and fruit.

Learn to embrace structure to find success. Build structures to support yourself and honour them with your commitment. Blessing the structures in your life will allow you to succeed.

POINTS TO REMEMBER

- The first chakra relates to the element of earth and everything that is solid and stable.

- Learning to ground ourselves will bring us stability and help with prosperity.

- The first chakra represents our physical identity, oriented to self-preservation.

- Our instincts are hard-wired to survival and keeping the body intact at all costs.

- The deep programming of the first chakra occurs in the first year of life, when survival needs are provided by parents. This creates safety.

- The first chakra rules the legs and feet, bones and teeth, diet and exercise.

- The demon of the first chakra is fear.

- The first-chakra principle is: "Push down to rise up."

- The deeper your roots, the higher you can reach.

Chakra Two

WATER

Chakra Two

Water

*The mind is like an iceberg. It floats with
one seventh of its bulk above water.*
SIGMUND FREUD

Location:	Lower back, abdomen, genitals
Name and meaning:	Svadhisthana, one's own place
Purposes:	Fluidity, movement, pleasure, feeling
Element:	Water
Principle:	Polarity
Developmental age:	6 months to 2 years
Identity:	Emotional identity
Orientation:	Self-gratification
Demon:	Guilt
Right:	To feel
Seed sound:	*Vam*
Colour:	Orange
Balanced form:	Fluid, graceful, satisfied

Diving into the waters

Entering the realm of chakra two opens up a watery world of feelings and emotions, sensations and desires, movement and juicy sexuality. The archetypal element shifts from earth to water, from solid to liquid. The stable ground developed in chakra one now "melts" into a flow of energy that begins its journey up the spine. The focus of consciousness expands from the single embodied self of chakra one to a nebulous world of duality, of *self and other*. Juicy indeed, this chakra can be as problematic as it is wonderful.

The essential purpose of this chakra is to stimulate movement and to bring pleasure into our lives. Moving our body through the outer world brings change, which stimulates consciousness and begins the awakening process. Physical movement, such as dancing, walking, or exercising, helps move the blood and lymph through the cells, or even purify the body through sweating, all through the element of water. Moving wakes up the energy body.

In the inner world, this chakra looks at what makes the subtle energy flow through the body. Internally, we are "moved" by strong emotion, perhaps brought about by a story or a poem, or an encounter with a friend. We can also stimulate the flow of energy through practices such as yoga or breathwork.

As the subtle energy begins its journey, it brings more feeling and sensation into the body, which in turn brings more vitality. As it moves, it may also push up against old pockets of blocked emotion and bring them back to life. Emotion, from the Latin *e*, meaning "out," and *movere*, "to move," moves our subtle energy up and out.

If the first-chakra challenges have been resolved, the focus of consciousness shifts from "What do I need in order to survive?" to "What do I *want* now that my survival is secure?" This can be as simple as completing our day of work and looking for something fun to do in the evening, or, on a deeper level, having solid enough financial ground to move in a new direction and follow our bliss.

Understanding the second-chakra symbol

The symbol of the second chakra is a six-petalled lotus containing a crescent moon. The moon signifies the pull of emotions on the subtle energy, much as the moon pulls the waters of the oceans to and fro with the tides. Much of this happens unconsciously, but an aspect of second-chakra work is to make the emotions conscious. I also think of this crescent moon, whose tips float upwards, as the "smile" of the second chakra – the smile of pleasure that comes when we are content and satisfied.

The animal associated with this chakra is the *makara*, a kind of fishlike crocodile that represents endless desire. To find balance in this chakra is to know which desires to satisfy and which will lead only to frustration and distraction from our spiritual path.

The seed sound in the centre of the chakra symbol is *Vam*.

The pleasure principle

Nature has placed mankind under the governance of two sovereign masters, pain and pleasure.
JEREMY BENTHAM

What gets *your* energy moving? If you are like most people, it comes down to a desire to make something different, hopefully for the better. That desire literally gets you up off your butt (first chakra) to move out into the world (second chakra). It may be as simple as wanting a glass of water or as complex as getting a medical degree. It may be a desire to connect with someone or to explore a new experience. We generally desire *to move towards pleasure and away from pain*. Pleasure is a major motivator that gets us moving.

Sigmund Freud called this the "pleasure principle" and claimed it was the essential motivator for *libido*, which is often equated with the sex drive. But libido is more than just the sex drive – it's also our general zest for life. If our life is dull and depressing, without anything to look forward to, our life-force will be lower than when we're excited about something. We may plod along, but there will be no motivation, nothing to get the life-force up and moving. And when there's chronic emotional or physical pain, the body shuts down sensation after a while, to avoid the experience. Without sensation, we become out of touch, disconnected from ourselves and others.

Belief systems that deny pleasure have led to a world of disconnection and numbness, with over-indulgence a compensation. Honouring the pleasure principle appropriately will bring joy to our life, life to our tissues, and motivation to our journey.

Emotional identity

We cannot selectively numb emotions. When we numb the painful emotions, we also numb the positive emotions.
Brené Brown

Tom and Janet sat in my office staring at each other in frustration. She wanted him to understand her feelings and to learn to communicate his own. But emotion was like a foreign language to Tom, one he had never learned to speak. While he was a dynamic character who "knew who he was" in his role as CEO of a successful technology firm, he had never developed an emotional identity and literally could not identify his own feelings, let alone hers. It wasn't that he didn't feel – he just didn't have the vocabulary to communicate his feelings to others. Instead they swirled around inside him, leaving him confused and disconnected. And the more they swirled, the more he shut down and became inaccessible to Janet.

The second chakra relates to our *emotional identity*, which is oriented to *self-gratification*. Here consciousness routinely scans our emotional state to see how we are feeling. Are we happy or sad, frightened or mad? We experience this all through the realm of *feeling*.

Emotions signal on a subconscious level whether something feels right or wrong, good or bad, pleasurable or painful. What we call "positive emotions," such as joy or excitement, are generally a desire to move *towards* something – the subconscious' way of saying, "Yes, I want this." What we often call "negative emotions," such as anger or fear, are a desire to move *away* from something or to move it out of our life. We might be angry about something that happened, sad about something we lost, or afraid that something bad might happen, but all are expressing some kind of dislike.

When our emotional state is pleasant, we generally don't try to change it. The emotional brain hums along and the body gets the message that everything is OK. We call this "contentment" or "satisfaction." It's a kind of wellbeing that allows energy to move forwards freely.

If the emotional state is not pleasant, however, it grabs our attention, begging to be changed. If we wake up depressed, for example, we might call a friend or therapist, we might go and get drunk, or we might try to find some other way to feel better. If that doesn't meet with success and the unpleasant state is lasting, we may choose to feel better by numbing our feelings or shutting down the second chakra. Then we disconnect from our emotional identity, and in doing so, lose touch with our capacity to bond emotionally.

So, we like to keep the positive emotions, and ideally use the negative emotions as a signal to change something in our lives. If the negative emotions cannot eventually do that, then our emotions get stuck, and eventually shut down.

Our ability to identify what we are feeling is directly related to keeping ourselves in a state of feeling that is as good as possible. With Tom and Janet, I helped him identify sensations in his body as a starting-point for getting to his emotions. He could at least say, "I feel tight in my belly," or "My jaw is clenching." Later we worked towards identifying some of those feelings as fear or anger. But Janet needed to learn to validate her own emotions, and look less towards Tom for doing that. As she learned to do this, Tom felt that he had a lot more space to explore his own feelings.

Developmental stage of the second chakra

Little Jenny had just learned to walk and now she was getting into everything – touching everything, putting things in her mouth and incessantly playing with noisy toys. "I can't take my eyes off her for a minute!" her mother stated with exasperation, running after her daughter yet again to take something out of her mouth that didn't belong there. "She's so emotional, and she cries when I take something away, but it doesn't last. A few minutes later she's off into something else, completely over it."

I smiled, as I knew this was entirely appropriate at this age. Jenny was in the second-chakra developmental stage, which takes place as a child moves from infant to toddler, at about six months to two years. Overlapping the first-chakra developmental phase of womb to one year, this stage starts when the child begins to sit upright. At this time, the visual acuity of the eyes shifts from the short focus on the mother's face to noticing details that are farther away – which brings the outer world into view. Of course this stimulates curiosity, which in turn stimulates the desire to move. First creeping, then crawling, then running, the child is soon getting into everything and experiencing the world through their senses.

Is everything that the child experiences going to be pleasant? Is everything going to be painful? No, the world is a mixed bag – a combination of pleasure and pain, good and bad, likes and dislikes. Ideally, the parent tries to protect the child from painful experiences as much as possible, and tries to enhance the good ones, laying down tracks in the memory that create an underlying feeling of wellbeing. But even the best parent has to say, "No, you can't have more ice cream," or, "No, you can't play with that knife." Sometimes the child finds their mother in a good mood and sometimes cross or unavailable. Pleasure and pain are the inevitable results of exploring a wider vista.

At this stage Jenny is learning to move towards pleasure and away from pain. She is experiencing her surroundings through her senses: she sees something, tastes it, touches it, smells, or hears it. This gives her an internal map of what is outside her.

She doesn't know much about the world, but she is learning through the realm of *feeling* whether something is pleasant or unpleasant. This is giving her the ground for her emotional identity and the flow of graceful movement in her body. It is setting the ground for her capacity for pleasure and ability to feel deeply.

And how does she communicate to others during this stage? Not with words, but through an expression of emotion – crying, screaming, laughing, smiling. If the adults around her respond properly to her emotions, then she learns to identify those emotions. She develops an "emotional literacy" and can later identify and name what she's feeling.

If this stage goes well, she will develop a healthy and balanced second chakra, with emotional depth, sensitivity, ease of movement and appropriate yet rewarding sexuality as an adult. If things do not go well at this stage, she may react by becoming excessive or deficient in this chakra, or a combination of both.

Excess and deficiency in the second chakra

Connie was a sensitive, emotional being. In fact, I'd say she only felt real when she was experiencing strong emotion. But her emotions were not always pleasant. Sometimes she was upbeat and happy, while at other times she had mood swings that took her down into depression, tears, and especially anger, much to the chagrin of those around her. She was overly identified with what she was feeling, once even declaring to her neighbour how powerful she felt when she was angry while simultaneously yelling at her over the fence.

Cecily was overly identified with her longings. She just couldn't resist the temptation of high-calorie foods like muffins and cakes, and she had a hard time resisting buying something she liked, even when she couldn't afford it. In relationships, she tended to be clingy, and she loved to touch and cuddle. Her partner, initially drawn to this, eventually found it draining to satisfy her needs.

Both Connie and Cecily showed signs of second-chakra excess. Connie wasn't drawn to satisfy her senses, but her emotions. Cecily actually sublimated her emotions through eating and shopping, so she showed her excess in sensory indulgence and a clinging attachment to others.

By contrast, people who are under-identified or deficient in the second chakra don't even know what they're feeling. Consequently, they may have trouble understanding or empathizing with the feelings of others. This was the case with Tom, mentioned above, who, logically enough, was married to a woman who was more excessive in her second chakra – and wanted emotional connection! It was as if he had just tuned out that channel, shut it down, and decided to live his life on other frequencies. It was only a problem when he entered into a relationship and his wife complained of not being "met where she lived" – in excessive emotion. Some version of this problem is fairly typical in relationships.

A person can actually be both excessive and deficient in this chakra, but in different aspects. I've seen people who were excessive emotionally but shut down sexually, and others who were just the opposite – highly sexual but shut down emotionally. Remember that both are just strategies to either avoid or compensate for wounds that were inflicted long ago. They may have become normal for the person involved, yet they have taken them out of balance.

People with excessive emotion and desire in the second chakra need to learn containment. These urges cannot be allowed to run the show, as they contain excessive charge from the past that can negatively affect the present. Those with deficient second chakras, however, need to learn to feel by thawing out what is frozen. A person under-identified with their emotions needs to validate what they are feeling, pay attention to the subtle sensations in their body, feel the currents of energy moving, and gradually allow that awareness to inform their emotional expression. In short, they need permission to *feel*. And remember, it is possible to exhibit both excessive and deficient qualities, even in the same chakra.

Excessive and deficient qualities in the second chakra

Excessive qualities	Deficient qualities	Balanced qualities
Overly emotional	Out of touch with emotions	Emotionally connected
Self-indulgent	Avoids pleasure, relaxation	Capacity for deep pleasure
Seductive	Prudish	Healthy boundaries
Addictive personality	Overly strict, punishing	Ability to embrace change
Overly sensitive	Numb	Ability to feel deeply but not get lost in emotions
Obsessive attachment	Lacks desire, passion, excitement	Nurturing to self and others
Loose body and pelvis	Rigid body	Graceful movement
Highly sexual	Non-sexual	Sexuality and sensuality balanced

The demon of guilt

Listening to Alice, it felt as though she couldn't win, no matter what she did. If she started her morning by going to the gym for a full workout, she felt guilty for not getting to work earlier. But if she went straight to work, she felt guilty for not exercising. If she ate something "naughty," she felt guilty, and if she took time for herself at the end of her workday, she felt guilty that she wasn't there for her children.

Alice wasn't guilty about some terrible thing she had done in the past. Her guilt was more subtle than that. She felt guilty about everything in her daily life, and this guilt kept her from enjoying what she was doing. As a result, she had no satisfaction or pleasure at all. This in turn, led to a tendency to overindulge in food and sleep, which made her feel – well, terribly guilty!

Guilt is the demon of the second chakra. Guilt says, "I shouldn't feel this way, I shouldn't be so angry or scared, or so insecure." Guilt says, "I shouldn't want that, I shouldn't need this." Guilt says, "I shouldn't have that desire, that sexual fantasy." Guilt says, "I'm not good enough, pure enough, righteous enough, or generous enough." Guilt can ruin any activity by keeping us from enjoying what we're doing and really being there while we're doing it.

Of course there are times we really *should* feel guilty about something. It is normal to feel guilty about harming ourselves or another person, being thoughtless or cruel, or going against our higher judgement. This kind of guilt allows us to examine our behaviour and make changes or amends. But the kind of free-flowing guilt that I saw in Alice stops the flow of energy that is the fluidity of the second chakra. It takes us out of our feelings, out of connection, and blocks enjoyment.

Exercise: Examine your guilt

• Make a list of all the things you feel guilty about.

• Notice when they come up during the day and what happens as a result.

• Notice what happens when guilt takes over. How present are you with what you are doing? How connected are you to others?

• What do you really want? What do you really need?

Physical exercises for the second chakra

Exercise: Rock the pelvis

• Lie on your back on a firm surface, like a floor or rug. Bend both your knees, placing your feet hip-width apart within 30 centimetres (1 foot) of your buttocks.

• With a rapid push and release motion, push your feet into the ground and release them, allowing this movement to rock your pelvis back and forth. Allow the rocking to be effortless, using only the muscles of your legs to rock the pelvis. Make sure your belly muscles are completely relaxed and you are only pushing with the legs.

• Notice how this relaxes stiffness in the lower back.

Exercise: Butterfly the legs

- Bring the soles of your feet together and your knees out to the side. Take a few deep breaths, bringing your awareness to your inner thighs and groin area.

- Inhale deeply, and as you exhale, slowly bring your knees together, allowing the movement to last as long as the breath.

- As you inhale, slowly move the legs apart.

- Repeat several times, coordinating your movement with your breath and allowing your breaths to be slow and deep.

- After a minute or so of moving slowly, pick up the pace, yet still move your knees together as you exhale and apart as you inhale.

- You may notice an increase of energy and sensation in your groin area. Notice how this feels. This is a great warm-up for sex, but if that is not appropriate or available, you can just stretch and move to distribute the energy throughout the whole body.

Exercise: Stand and rock

- Begin with the grounding stance (*see page 45*). *Place* your feet shoulder-width apart, in slightly pigeon-toed style, and inhale as you bend your knees and exhale as you push the floor away.

- When you begin to feel a little trembling in the legs, allow that energy to move into the second chakra by adding the following hip movements: as you inhale and bend your knees, increase the curve of your lower back, taking your tailbone as far back as possible. As you exhale and straighten your legs, press your hips and pubic bone forwards.

- Repeat several times, imagining that your pelvic floor is swaying forwards and backwards smoothly, like a swing.

- If you want to discharge energy (good for second-chakra excess) then put more emphasis into pressing your hips forwards, even snapping them rapidly.

- If you want to bring more energy into your second chakra to bring it alive (good for second-chakra deficiency), put more emphasis on bringing your tailbone to the back, rounding your lower belly, and curving your sacral area. Experiment and see what works for you.

POINTS TO REMEMBER

- The second chakra rules the hips, inner thighs, pelvis, sexual organs, womb, and fluid systems of the body, such as the urinary system.

- The importance of the second chakra is to get things moving freely and fluidly, like water, and to bring pleasure into our lives.

- The movement of energy is both internal and external.

- Pleasure and desire are primary motivators to get things moving.

- This chakra gives us our emotional identity, which is oriented to self-gratification. It wants us to feel good.

- The stage in which the second chakra is primarily developed is six months to two years. This is a highly emotional stage when a child is learning to move out into the world and communicate through their emotions.

- The demon of this chakra is guilt.

- Getting your energy moving is the best way to free up the second chakra, especially moving the hips and thighs.

Chakra Three

FIRE

Chakra Three

Fire

Mastering others is strength.
Mastering yourself is true power.
LAO TZU

Location:	Solar plexus
Name and meaning:	Manipura, lustrous gem
Purposes:	Energy, strength, purpose
Element:	Fire
Principle:	Combustion
Developmental age:	18 months to 3½ years
Identity:	Ego identity
Orientation:	Self-definition
Demon:	Shame
Right:	To act
Seed sound:	*Ram*
Colour:	Yellow/gold
Balanced form:	Strong, centred mastery

Finding your power

Power. It runs our world. From kings and queens to elected politicians, from money to the military, from divine power to the electricity that fuels our homes, power is evident in every aspect of life. How to handle that power, both personally and collectively, is a major question of our times. From the one to the many, evolution itself is a quest for the ability to do more with less, to combat the powerlessness of being a single agent, to harnessing the power to create change.

Raised into obedience, where power is seen as something outside ourselves, vested in authority figures, parents, teachers, priests, bosses, or politicians, life for many of us becomes a constant quest for power. We begin as children, powerless before our parents, knowing little about the world. We grow up through school systems, religions, perhaps the military, and go out and find our place in the world. We start in entry-level jobs and work our way up, hoping to achieve enough power simply to determine our own lives. And we discover that power dynamics enter into every relationship, from intimate to professional, and that our programming around power affects every decision we make.

Power is the subject of chakra three, located in the solar plexus. You know that place: it's where you feel butterflies in your belly whenever you get nervous. It's that place in the gut that tightens up when you don't know what to do. Or that place that simply collapses when your energy is low and everything feels like too much.

The solar plexus has no bones in the front of it, only soft tissue, which is why holding ourselves upright requires *backbone* – a word that also connotes standing up for ourselves, being willing to face conflict, or holding our power. If the third chakra is too empty, the solar plexus doesn't fill and the body collapses around it. If it is too full, we become rigid, dense, bloated, or trapped at this chakra level.

Power is energy, so it is no surprise that *fire* is the element connected with the third chakra, Manipura, whose name means "lustrous gem." After consolidating our physical vehicle in chakra one and getting our vehicle moving in chakra two, we have to learn how to keep that vehicle energized, so we can steer it and avoid hitting obstacles along the way. For that, we need energy, power, and will. How does the body create these aspects of the third chakra?

Rub your palms together briskly for 30 seconds or more. What happens? It creates heat. The longer you do it, the more warmth you create. This illustrates the principle of how energy is generated from the combination of chakra one and chakra two. Chakra one is matter – your hands – and chakra two is movement – rubbing your palms against each other. The result is friction, which in turn creates heat. Rubbing two sticks together creates fire, and friction in any machinery creates heat and requires energy. So it takes energy to create energy, but once the fire gets going, it's easier to generate energy.

Waking up the third chakra is about igniting your internal fire, strengthening your will, and applying all that to a purpose. It comes from getting the body moving, overcoming inertia, and directing the energy within you towards a goal.

Understanding the third-chakra symbol

The third-chakra symbol is a lotus of 10 petals, representing the 10 fingers of the hands, our way of making things happen in the world. The root of the word "manipulate," "man," means "hand." We think of manipulation as a bad thing, but in truth we are manipulating matter into energy all the time, through the food we eat, the things we move around, and the actions we take.

Inside the lotus is a downward-pointing triangle, indicating, just as in the first chakra, that our focal point rises from the Earth and expands as we move upwards. The goddess Shakti (primordial energy) is also denoted by a triangle, whose three phases at this chakra combine the aspects of will, action, and knowledge (in Sanskrit *Iccha*, *Kriya*, and *Jnana*). It's not enough to have will and action alone – they must be tempered by knowledge or consciousness. There are many trinities in Hinduism as well: the three *gunas*, or qualities, *Tamas*, *Rajas*, and *Sattvas*, or matter, energy, and consciousness, and the triple aspects of the gods and goddesses as creators, preservers, and destroyers. Power comes from the wise combination of all these trinities, rising above the dualities of the second chakra.

Inside the lotus is a ram, the animal of power, and the seed sound symbol, which is *Ram*.

Think of this whole symbol as a lustrous gem, powerfully shining out from your solar plexus and firing up your power.

Strengthening the will

> *The most common way people give up their power is by thinking they don't have any.*
> ALICE WALKER

Power comes from a clear and deliberate personal will – one that is not so strong that it dominates others but not so weak that it is dominated by others. Let's look at the relationship between energy and will.

Children have lots of energy. They run around, make noise, and play hard, with little thought about what they are doing. Adults are often the opposite: they do what they must, carrying out their duties and honouring their responsibilities (that almost defines an adult), but tend to run out of energy as they get older. Successful strengthening of the will combines the energy from below with the consciousness from above.

We have stated that energy is the fuel for the third chakra and is made from combining matter and movement, aspects of chakras one and two. But to truly develop our power, we must have a strong will. Will is the combination of energy, rising up from the lower chakras for the purpose of *action*, and consciousness, descending from the crown chakra, which provides the *intention*. Action without intention is merely whim and can even be harmful. Intention without action – well, we know there's a very famous road paved with those intentions. It leads to nothing but powerlessness.

Will directs our energy into our intention to produce a desired outcome. We may have the intention to stick to a diet, get up and meditate, or clean the house, but if we don't have the energy to do so, the intention is but a mere thought; it remains unmanifest. Or we may have lots of energy to do something but we don't know quite what to do, or perhaps how to do it.

When intention and energy successfully combine and we accomplish what we set out to do, we have a sense of power. Think of the way you feel when you cross off a big item on your to-do list, turning your "to-do" into a "Tada!" From that feeling of power, you get a sense of self-esteem. You say, "I can do that!" which makes you more confident about managing your life.

This is the role of the third chakra: to combine the downward current of consciousness with the rising current of energy to form a strong will that can channel that energy into effective action. This means our energy and intention need to be in alliance and harmony. When they want to go in different directions, such as the energy wanting to stay in bed and the intention to get up and meditate, then we become blocked in the third chakra. It simply doesn't know what to do, because it's getting conflicting impulses from different parts of us.

The long-term goal of the third chakra is *mastery* – mastery of our energy body, mastery of our emotions, actions, words, and thoughts. Mastery arises through years of practice, and practice is the result of combining energy and intention – over and over again – until it becomes effortless. True power is found in the ease that comes from effortless mastery.

Mastery is not control, however, which is one part asserting power *over* another, nor is it controlling others through domination. Mastery is aligning with an inner guidance system, the effective and deliberate steering of our vehicle along the path of our destiny.

Desire and will

While it's wonderful to be in the second-chakra waters that follow the path of least resistance towards pleasure, there are always aspects of life and work that are not entirely pleasurable. Whenever we make a commitment – to show up at a job every day, to raise a child, to stay in a marriage – there are days when our desires and feelings don't match our commitment. We simply don't feel like going to work one day, we'd rather stay in bed than get our child off to school, or we have trouble remembering why we ever married that person across from us at the breakfast table. At those times, we need a strong will to power through.

When we go through the second chakra, we encounter desire and choice. "Do I want to go this way or that way?" "Do I want to approach or avoid?" When we actively make a choice and take action to obtain it, then we are engaging the will.

But desire and will have a strange relationship. They are not always in alignment and can even be enemies of each other. When a choice comes up – what *should* we do versus what we *want* to do – desire and will are like two horses racing to get out of the starting-gate. If we indulge our desires too much, the will gets lazy, and desire wins out. We have a hard time doing what we need to do, whether it's washing the dishes, finishing our work, or sticking to a discipline such as working out or dieting.

But when the will is too strong and dominates desire, we start to lose our zest for life. We move away from the pleasure of things, and life becomes dull and plodding. We start to lose the energy coming up from the lower two chakras, and then there isn't much fuel for the will.

Ideally, will and desire are in alignment, and then the desire feeds the will. Think of how you feel when you get up early to go on vacation, compared to getting up early to go to work. Same task, but you have more enthusiasm when desire is present.

It's important to remember that we are always choosing. If the talk going on inside our head is nothing but a series of "have-tos" – "I have to clean the house," "I have to pay the bills" – then we put power outside ourselves and lose the sense of choice. If we rephrase our inner dialogue to reflect *choice*, then we empower ourselves. We can say, "I choose to do the dishes because I want a clean kitchen." Sticking to a diet, for example, then becomes a matter of choosing to eat healthy, nutritious food instead of starving ourselves and feeling deprived.

Strengthening the will begins with realizing that everything we are doing – even if we think it is only to please someone else – we are actually doing with our will. Owning our will is the first step to reclaiming it, and the first step to power.

Exercise: Make a list

- Make a list of everything you tell yourself you "have to" do. Include short-term things like cleaning the house and longer-term things like finishing a project or doing your taxes. Here's an example:

    I have to:

    - Do the laundry.
    - Write this report.
    - Be nicer to my neighbour.
    - Pay my bills.
    - Wash the dishes.
    - Spend more time with my kids.
    - Clean out the garage.
    - Lose some weight.
    - Eat better.
    - Exercise more.

- Your list might be quite long. Notice how that feels.

- Then reread the list, change all your "have-tos" to "choose to" and notice how that feels. You might even put "choose to because..." as in "I choose to pay my bills because I want to keep a good credit score," "I choose to eat better because it makes me feel good."

Notice we are not going all the way to "want to." That may never be the case with your taxes or bills, but you can still empower yourself by choosing. And if you can't "choose" what you are doing, then you might question why you are doing it.

Remember, you can also choose *not* to do something. Saying "no" to what you don't want is also the realm of the will.

Developmental stage of the third chakra

My friend Karen was exasperated. Her son, Nathan, was in his terrible twos and very difficult to manage. At every turn he thwarted her will, saying "no," throwing temper tantrums, and generally refusing to cooperate. She was at her wits' end.

Every parent remembers the difficulty of this third-chakra stage, when the child finds their own will and uses it like a new toy to manipulate everyone around them. While it is good to develop strength of will, a child knows very little about the world, so cannot use it appropriately. They don't know that it's not safe to play in the street, that eating too many sweet things makes you sick, and that there will be a lot of angry stares if they scream in the grocery store.

If the first chakra is about holding on and the second chakra is about letting go, then the third chakra is about knowing *when to hold on and when to let go.* This plays out in whether to let out your feelings or hold them in, whether to speak or remain silent, whether to take action or sit back. In childhood, however, it is most apparent in the task of toilet training, which is learning when to hold on and when to let go.

The developmental task here is *impulse control.* Prior to the third-chakra stage, children are little reaction machines: what goes in comes right out, both literally and figuratively. They cry when they're sad and scream when they're frustrated, with little regard for the consequences, simply because prior to this stage they don't have the muscular or mental maturity to control their own behaviour.

In order to become socialized, however (which happens at the heart chakra, above this one), Nathan will have to learn to control his impulses to hit, steal, yell, break things, or emotionally dominate. But for most children at this stage, their energy wants to go straight into action! The world is a playground to be explored and relished. Thus the parent and child engage in a battle of wills that lasts throughout most of this stage, from about 18 months to three years (and may return at adolescence!)

When Nathan does control his impulses, he generally gets rewarded or appreciated. He also has his first experience of mastery, which, as you remember, builds self-esteem. When Nathan has a sense of being able to master a task, such as getting dressed or putting a toy together, he develops self-confidence. A child must have a sense of power to gain confidence, but that power must be developed in balance with the power of other people.

The trouble is, some parents expect too much of their child, or too much too soon. Then the child has a hard time experiencing any mastery at all, and the third chakra remains depleted or deficient. Children overly controlled by authoritarian parents must so deeply deny their own impulses that their spontaneity and playfulness disappear. Yet still other children are so heavily indulged by their parents that they get a false sense of their own power and later have a hard time getting on with others.

Ego identity

It is at this stage that the child begins to develop their ego identity, which is oriented to self-definition. The ego gives us our first sense of self, of who we are and how we want to show up in the world. We need a strong ego to survive in this competitive world. We need to know who we are and what we're up to, and to be able to defend ourselves if necessary.

The ego is like an executive identity: it decides what the game plan is going to be and how to execute it. But the ego is not the whole person, and getting stuck at this level traps us in our ego identity and keeps us from getting to the upper chakras, especially the heart chakra.

Ideally, the ego is like a house. It's where we have clothes that are our size, our favourite art on the walls, and our kind of food in the refrigerator. We need a house or apartment to come home to after a hard day's work. But if we never left our home, we would lead a very small life indeed. There is a big world out there – much bigger than our little ego.

Having a strong ego is appropriate for a healthy third chakra. But getting trapped here will keep us from advancing spiritually, missing out on more than half the chakra system yet to come! It's important to let the ego know it has an appropriate place, but keeping it in its place is equally important.

The demon of shame

A shame-based person will guard against exposing his inner self to others, but more significantly, he will guard against exposing himself to himself.
JOHN BRADSHAW

We have stated that the ultimate goal of third-chakra power is self-mastery. When we successfully combine our energy and our intention to create a desired outcome, we feel powerful.

The flipside of that is the third-chakra demon of shame. Shame is the opposite of power. Shame tends to collapse the third chakra and make us want to hide or withdraw. It can paralyse us with the fear of doing something wrong or it can make us overwork in order to prove ourselves worthy.

Parents too often shame their children over their naturally immature actions. "What's the matter with you? You should be ashamed of yourself!" Or, "I'm so ashamed of you because of what you've done. How do you think that makes me feel?"

When this happens the child associates their natural tendency to turn energy into action as dangerous. When energy does come out, it is judged and shamed. "That wasn't good enough." "I'm always messing things up." "I can't do anything right." Then the energy becomes bound up inside and may be hard to access at all later on. Alternatively, however, some people react to a shaming past by doubling their efforts to prove themselves, resulting in overdoing and exhaustion. These are examples of excess and deficiency in the third chakra, both of which can result from this insidious demon.

Excess and deficiency in the third chakra

Mary Lou sat in my office, slumped and contracted, tears streaming down her face. She told me that she was in a state of panic over a presentation she had to do the next day. She was terrified of stepping out and being seen, terrified of failing, and had a past pattern of not following through with her will when she set out to do something. Her third chakra was completely collapsed, and when I had her stand up and push her solar plexus into my hand, I could feel that there was simply no substance there. It was as if I could push all the way back to her spine, with no resistance. No wonder she was scared! Mary Lou had a deficient third chakra.

Ron, in contrast, was a powerhouse. The owner of a large company, he worked long hours and had lots of responsibility. He made a good living for his family, but his habit of controlling everything around him, including himself, was now putting a strain on his marriage. His wife was threatening to leave if he didn't make some big changes, slow down, and learn how to create intimacy. This was the most difficult thing Ron had ever been asked. He had an excessive third chakra.

Excess in the third chakra can also take the form of simply *doing too much*. One becomes a human doing instead of a human being, perhaps less concerned about controlling circumstances or other people yet always trying to accomplish something. This serves the ego identity of the third chakra, which is seeking self-esteem. In Western culture, we are rewarded for accomplishment, and this can lead to excessive activity – but eventually run the third chakra into exhaustion.

Excessive and deficient qualities in the third chakra

Excessive qualities	Deficient qualities	Balanced qualities
Controlling	Weak-willed	Assertive
Dominating	Victim mentality	Deliberate
Constantly active	Passive	Self-disciplined
Ulcers, heartburn	Poor digestion	Good digestion
Temperature on the warm side	Temperature on the cool side	Warm
Arrogant	Low energy	Confident
Stubborn	Blaming	Courageous
Driven	Aimless	Purposeful

Exercise: Building up power

In order to feel powerful, we need to move energy through our body deliberately. This exercise is best done with another person, but if alone, you can use a wall instead.

- Stand in front of another person with your elbows bent at your sides and your palms facing up and away from you. Make sure your hands are at third-chakra height, which means your forearms are more or less parallel to the floor. (Alternately, press your palms into a wall, with your forearms parallel to the floor and your hands at third-chakra height.)

- Facing your partner, place your palms against theirs (or place your palms against the wall). Ground yourself and connect up and down through your core, *staying in the centre line of your energy*.

- From this line, push forwards into your partner's hands (or the wall), without losing your alignment through your core. Be careful to stay in alignment and avoid leaning forwards from your core. Make sure your torso stays vertical. Simply push your arms forwards *from* the core. Imagine the way a tree pushes a branch out from its trunk, but doesn't push the trunk forwards.

- As you push into your partner's hands, they push into yours at the same time. (The wall is just neutral, but solid and provides resistance.)

- Open your eyes and look at the other person. Each of you is in your power and meeting the other in their power. Hold your power, even allowing yourself to growl or make a face if you wish.

- Then gradually ease off the pressure in your hands and slowly disengage. Bring your hands to your belly and feel the power there.

- Share your experience with your partner.

Exercise: Woodchopper

They say that he who cuts his own wood is warmed twice, once by the fire and once by the action of chopping wood. This exercise will make you warm. It gets your third chakra loose and moving. It's good for discharging the third chakra, but also for letting go of stagnation and blockages.

- Stand with your feet shoulder-width apart and slightly bend your knees. Take a few breaths in and out, practising the grounding technique (*see page 45*), i.e. inhaling as you bend your knees and exhaling as you push the floor away and straighten your legs.

- When you get some energy moving in your legs, add the second-chakra piece (*see page 72*), which is to take your tailbone back as you inhale and bend your knees, and move your hips forwards as you exhale and straighten your legs.

- Now you are ready to bring the energy you have generated up into the third chakra. Widen your stance, moving your feet wider apart than your shoulders. Raise your arms up overhead, interlacing your fingers and slightly arching your back, taking your wrists slightly behind you.

- Inhale fully and imagine you are holding an axe between your hands and there is a block of wood in front of you.

- When you are ready, exhale with a loud "hah" sound and move your wrists and entire torso down towards the imaginary block of wood. Allow your wrists to move all the way down between your legs to slightly behind you. Allow your head to follow.

- Inhale and rise to a standing position again, arms overhead.

- "Charge up again," and repeat several times, each time coming down with a smooth swoosh and a loud "hah" sound.

- When you have finished, pause and feel the area around your third chakra. It should feel warm, somewhat freer, and more relaxed.

POINTS TO REMEMBER

- The third chakra's element is fire.

- We create energy by combining matter and movement.

- Will is the combination of energy and intention.

- We develop self-esteem through mastery, and mastery through practice.

- Shame is the demon of the third chakra and collapses the solar plexus.

- We need an ego to succeed, but do not want to be trapped by it.

- Balancing excess and deficiency creates effective power.

Chakra Four

AIR

Chakra Four

Air

*Your task is not to seek for love, but to
seek and find all the barriers within yourself
that you have built against love.*
RUMI

Location:	Chest, lungs, and heart
Name and meaning:	Anahata, unstruck sound
Purposes:	Love, balance, spaciousness
Element:	Air
Principle:	Equilibrium
Developmental age:	3½–7 years
Identity:	Social identity
Orientation:	Self-acceptance
Demon:	Grief
Right:	To love and be loved
Seed sound:	*Yam*
Colour:	Green
Balanced form:	Open, loving, centred

The mysterious essence of love

Each of the chakras opens us not only to a place inside ourselves but to a realm of being. In the heart chakra, that realm is the field of universal love. We are enveloped in that field, but too often we cannot see it, just as we are enveloped in a field of air, yet it remains invisible. And, like the air, which is the element of the heart chakra, we cannot live without love. We take it in with each breath, inhaling and exhaling it in constant exchange. To open to that love, both within and without, and to find the place where inner and outer worlds connect, that is the task of the heart chakra.

How do we open the heart? How do we find our way to more love, to deeper love, to wider love? How do we open ourselves to receiving love, to loving ourselves unconditionally? And from that opening, how do we give more love, enhancing those around us, helping our world awaken to the possibilities of a love-based paradigm.

We find love within ourselves through connecting to the core of our being. It requires tuning in to the body (chakra one), allowing the flow of feeling (chakra two), supporting ourselves with a calm and steady will (chakra three), and then, with the support of the lower chakras, opening to the spaciousness of air at the heart.

The heart, then, is the very centre of our being. We have three chakras above it and three chakras below, so it is the place of balance and integration.

Just as the third chakra focuses energy into "doing," the heart chakra takes us to a state of profound "being." Rising above will and effort, we surrender to a higher power, a wider opening, an expansive softness, balancing giving and receiving in perpetual reciprocity. Yet will is often needed to arrive at that state of being, much as the effort of climbing a mountain is necessary to get to the top, where we take off our pack, relax, and enjoy just being there. When the third chakra has done its work, the heart chakra is supported in its opening.

Then we find love all around us as we appreciate the incredible blessings of life, with all its beauty, mystery, magic, and infinite variety. Even our lessons, hard as they sometimes are, open us to compassion, forgiveness, understanding, and love. These attributes of the heart soften the body – soften the boundary between inner and outer, the self and the other – so that we open to the love that is there all the time.

The universal field of love that is all around us is both intelligent and compassionate. It is ready to embrace us, to bestow its countless blessings. It is waiting for us to realize it's been there all along, guiding us, blessing us, loving us. We need only melt away the barriers we've built in self-protection, barriers that might have felt necessary at some time in the past, but now only get in our way.

Love is the glue of the universe, holding our world together in a myriad of relationships perpetually exchanging energy with each other. It is this exchange that makes the whole world possible, from the trees breathing out oxygen and breathing in carbon dioxide, to the mushrooms that break down plants into soil, to the sun and rain that need just the right balance to create life. It is a profound miracle that this world holds together as well as it does.

If sex is the first place we experience a dissolution of the ego bubble that keeps us separate, then falling in love is the place where that dissolution becomes more permanent than a momentary experience. As we climb up through the chakras, heading towards the unity of universal consciousness, falling and staying in love are essential steps to our awakening.

Exercise: Time to breathe!

- Take a deep breath. Feel the air filling your lungs, expanding your chest. Feel the spaciousness that is created with a deep inhalation. Perhaps even hold your breath for a moment while you hug your lower chakras tightly into your core.

- Now let the breath out again, gently releasing tensions in your body as you soften your shoulders, your chest, your arms, and hands.

- Feel the natural impulse to breathe in again, and allow your lungs to fill even more deeply. As you do so, imagine that your whole body is breathing, that your skin is a membrane that is expanding and contracting, that the boundary between inner and outer is softly dissolving...

- Notice the natural balance between breathing out and breathing in. There is always enough air to breathe in, always another breath to take, from your first gasp at birth to your last breath at the end of life. Like the heart that never stops beating from the womb to the tomb, the breath is the very hallmark of life.

Air, the element of the heart chakra, is lighter and freer than earth, water, or fire, the elements of the first three chakras. It is naturally expansive. It fills every space with its invisible essence. The room you are in right now is filled with air, evenly distributed throughout. Air fills a balloon and makes it expand, just as it fills our chest and creates expansion in the Inner Temple. Air nourishes every part of the body, as the heart beats oxygen into every cell. Air has no edges and boundaries – you can't tell where a field of air stops or starts. Filling your chest with air creates spaciousness inside the body, an opening to a subtle emptiness that allows your being to expand.

To give the heart room to expand, it's necessary to create space and time for yourself. I write this from a remote island off the coast of western Canada, where I am taking a writing retreat. Meditating in the quiet stillness of the seaside retreat, I realize how busy my daily life is, how I'm constantly moving from one thing to another. As I open to the stillness, the breath softly flowing in and out of me, I am reminded of how little time I leave for emptiness, for just being, for softening to the field of universal love.

We talk about needing room to breathe. The heart chakra also requires a kind of spaciousness to open to the expanse of love, the presence of peace, and to the energy rising to pierce the chakras above.

Understanding the fourth-chakra symbol

The symbol of the heart chakra is a lotus of 12 petals that contains two intersecting triangles, making a six-pointed star. These triangles represent the interpenetration of matter and spirit, with the lower moving to the higher and the higher moving to the lower: matter and spirit in perfect balance. Many people know the six-pointed star as the Star of David, a widely used symbol in the Jewish faith. Fewer people know that these intersecting triangles also represent the Sacred Marriage, the balance and integration of masculine and feminine, God and Goddess, inner and outer.

Inside the star is the seed sound of the heart chakra, which is *Yam*.

Its animal is an antelope, a gentle, horned creature that runs in the wild with tenderness and grace.

The 12 lotus petals of the heart chakra can have a number of associations: the 12 signs of the zodiac, the doubling of the second chakra's six petals, or the doubling of the six points of the star.

Just below the heart is a smaller sub-chakra, called the *Anandakanda* Lotus, which contains the Celestial Wishing Tree. It is believed that when you wish from the deepest desires of your heart, this tree bestows even *more* than is desired. So be careful what you wish for![2]

The Hindu monkey-headed god, Hanuman, is often depicted pulling open his heart chakra to reveal the god and goddess, Ram and Sita, intertwining in it. The story goes that Hanuman taught that Ram and Sita resided within everything, even his pearl necklace. The people around him said that was ridiculous, so Hanuman ripped open his chest to reveal the lovers there. Sometimes we have to rip ourselves open to feel the raw power of love.

---

2. For a meditation on the Celestial Wishing Tree, check out www. creatingonpurpose.net or the book *Creating on Purpose* by Anodea Judith and Lion Goodman, Sounds True, Boulder, CO, 2012.

Opening the heart

Allow things to come and go; keeping your heart as open as the sky.
LAO TZU

Everywhere I go, it seems people want to learn how to open their heart. If love is our natural state of being, why is this so difficult?

Linda, a quiet woman in her forties, was a case in point. She came to me feeling disconnected from her heart and from her soul. She complained of being tired and listless and feeling a bit lost. As I listened to her words, I also watched her breathing. I noticed that her inhalations were short and quick and that after each exhalation she waited for what seemed like a long time – a second or two – before she took the next breath. No wonder she felt empty! Her chest and belly had collapsed towards the back of the sofa and her shoulders had drooped, making it even more difficult to take in a deep breath.

Knowing Linda's background, I wasn't surprised. She had received very little nurturing as a young child, so there wasn't a lot to take in from her environment. As a result, her breathing matched her childhood experience of loneliness and isolation. However, that breathing pattern was now creating the same experience in her adult life.

I encouraged Linda to take her tailbone towards the back of her seat, to sit up straight, and to lift her chest, pressing her shoulders back and down. We did a couple of stretching exercises to open the chest (*see below*) and she began to brighten, as if she were becoming more present in the room. I then suggested she notice her natural breathing pattern and how she held herself empty for longer than she was full. I helped her explore the origins of that pattern, so she could release any emotions around it, especially those of grief – the demon of the heart chakra.

Once she had released some of her tears, her breathing naturally started to change. She spontaneously took a deep breath, not because she was forcing it, but because the grief that had been taking up space in her heart had been moved outwards and released. I had her follow her breath inwards and hold it for a moment to see what that felt like. As she exhaled, I taught her to take her next breath sooner than she had been previously, feeling the air as a field of infinitely compassionate, nurturing love.

Each breath she took transformed her. Her chest and face softened, and she felt that she was supplying herself with what she needed rather than trying to get it from outside. While it would take some weeks of practice before this new breathing pattern became a habit, she was on the road to a new experience of her heart.

Exercise: Opening the chest

The heart chakra sits squarely in the centre of the chest, even though the organ of the heart itself is just slightly to the left. Opening the chest creates more room for breath, which simultaneously creates more energy, more love, and more vitality.

- Stand with your feet hip-width apart, bending and straightening your knees a few times to establish your ground.

- Bring your hands over your heart and see if you can sense your heartbeat. (If not, you can place your fingers on the carotid artery just below your ears on either side of the neck; *see below*.)

- Breathe deeply into your chest, noticing if it takes an effort to take a deep breath or it comes naturally, or if you tend to hold on to the breath and not release it fully. Just notice your own breathing pattern for several breaths without trying to change it.

- Next, interlace your fingers behind your back. Roll your shoulders back and straighten your elbows, noticing how this lifts your chest and presses it forwards. (If this is too difficult, due to shoulder tension, you can put a strap or a cloth between your hands to widen the distance and make it easier.)

- As you lift your chest, press your wrists away from your spine while taking your head back slightly, extending your neck. Notice how this opens your chest even further.

- Take a deep breath into the space you are creating. Open your mouth wide to release the breath.

- The next step is to start to bow forwards from the hips, lengthening your spine while keeping your chest expanded, your hands interlaced and your elbows straight.

- As you bow forwards, release your entire upper body and allow your hands to fall naturally with gravity, moving away from your spine.

- Shake your head from side to side, making sure your neck is loose, and remain folded in this position for several breaths.

- To rise up again, lift your head and press your chest forwards, away from your hips.

- Slowly come to a standing position. Lift your chest again, then release your hands to your sides.

- Stand naturally and notice if you have a little more room to breathe and if your body feels more expansive.

Exercise: Arm circles

Loosening the shoulders is good for expanding the heart.

- Stand with your feet hip-width apart, firmly in your ground.

- Lift both arms horizontally, in a "T" shape, with your palms facing downwards.

- Press your fingertips upwards and push into the heels of your hands, expanding your energy from your heart down both your arms to the periphery of your fingertips.

- Next, relax your palms and begin to make circles with your arms, forwards, up and back. (This is clockwise on the right and counterclockwise on the left.) Begin with very small circles, then gradually make them wider and wider until you are making the largest circles possible for you. Make sure you are breathing as you do this, ideally breathing in as your arms are lifting and breathing out as they are falling behind you.

- Change direction and begin to make the circles slightly smaller, and then smaller and smaller until your arms press out again into a "T."

Exercise: Breath of joy

This exercise is fun to do as it gets the energy moving easily and effortlessly, loosens the torso, and energizes the heart. It involves three consecutive inhalations and one big exhalation.

- Stand with your feet at least hip-width apart and your knees slightly bent. Inhale and raise your arms forwards, then inhale again and move them to the side, then inhale and lift them overhead.

- Then exhale fully as you sweep your arms down and back, bending forwards as you do so.

- Inhale as you come to a standing position and repeat the three inhalations and the arm movements forwards, to the side, and upwards, exhaling again as you bring the arms down and bend forwards.

- Repeat several times, then stand with your eyes closed to feel the effects.

Developmental stage of the fourth chakra

Nathan, whom we met earlier, was finally moving out of his third-chakra stage. He had developed a sense of his own power and autonomy and was ready to enter the social world of relationships. Not that he hadn't been wanting and responding to love since his earliest beginnings, but until he had gained control of his impulses he couldn't do much about shaping his personality. But now he had gained enough self-control to shape his behaviour in ways that he thought would bring him love, attention, and approval.

This occurs in the family, in school, and in the neighbourhood. In some families, the child now has younger brothers or sisters, or perhaps is getting old enough to play with older brothers and sisters. Nathan was starting to play with children in the neighbourhood and getting ready to go to school. As children enter this uncertain realm of social interaction, it becomes very important to be liked and included by classmates and teachers.

What does a child do to gain approval at this stage? One child may learn that being quiet is a way to win love. Another may learn that it comes from being smart, funny, helpful, or good at sports. A little girl may learn how to be cute, a boy how to be strong and masculine, as they take their cues from people in the family, on the television, and in the environment.

All this is fine and dandy, except that often some of the messier parts of the child get repressed in this process. A child may learn that their needy part is something to be ashamed of and repress their needs lifelong. Another child may learn that they are rejected if they make too much noise or talk too much, and thus learn to be quiet and self-contained. A girl may learn she has to be pretty, and then feel insecure lifelong if she is not happy with her looks or her body. A boy may feel he has to act like a little man and repress his feelings of sadness or insecurity.

When we lose a part of ourselves, or the love of someone important, we feel sad. Grief is the demon of the heart chakra. It is heavy and sits on the heart chakra like a stone, whereas the energy of air is light and uplifting. But, like all demons, when we work through our grief, perhaps crying it out, our heart lightens like the sky after a rainstorm.

To combat grief, the adult work of the heart chakra seeks to reclaim some of the lost parts of ourselves and integrate them into our heart. Here's a little exercise for doing just that:

Exercise: Reclaiming a lost part

This exercise takes you through a number of introspective questions. It can be done with a friend or therapist, or, if one is not available, you can simply write the answers in your own journal. As you write or speak, be sure you take the time to really *feel* the process. It is not the intellectual answers to these questions that is important but the inner work triggered by the enquiry itself.

- What do you like best about yourself? (It always helps to begin with appreciating something positive.) How does it feel in your body when you appreciate that part of yourself?

- What do you find hardest to love about yourself? What do you judge or feel ashamed of? Notice how it feels in your body to focus on that part of yourself.

- When did you develop that trait? What age? Look back on your life and name some of the forces that were acting upon you at the time.

Examples might be:

- I was the only child and then suddenly I had a younger brother.

- I was responsible for my family at a young age.

- I had a violent father who scared and hurt me.

- My family moved around frequently and I had to keep starting over in a new school and make new friends.

- My mother wasn't very nurturing and was often angry at all of us kids.

- Examine the trait you don't like in light of these forces. Imagine you can talk to that part of yourself, saying something like, "Now I understand why you're here and what you were trying to do."

- Forgive that part of yourself and thank it for trying to take care of you.

- After forgiveness has occurred, make a place inside your heart chakra for this part of yourself. You might imagine a special chair or cushion for it to sit upon. You might see it as your inner three-year-old or five-year-old. Imagine that there is a sacred place in your heart just for that little person.

- Notice how all of this feels in your body and anchor those sensations by grounding into your body. If desired, pick another trait that you judge.

- BONUS! Once you have done this with yourself, you can do it with another person. If another person has a trait that you find difficult, ask them how and why that trait was created. Once you understand their story, you may find it easier to forgive them for having that trait. And strangely enough, with that forgiveness, the trait may become less present!

Excess and deficiency in the fourth chakra

It's hard to imagine having too much love in your heart, so excess and deficiency in this chakra get a little tricky. What's important to remember is that both states are the result of defences around a previous wound. A deficient chakra is the result of avoiding something and an excessive chakra is the result of compensating for something – doing too much.

In the heart chakra, the deficient response is fairly obvious, as in the case of Charles. He was brought in to see me by his wife, who complained that he avoided intimacy and connection – something she wanted more of. A little digging into Charles' story revealed that he was quite introverted. Most of his life he had avoided relationships, preferring to focus on his work, which was both intellectual and demanding. He described himself as a loner who had always shied away from social situations and never found it easy to make close friends. At base, he was mostly just shy, and had never felt easy or comfortable forming relationships.

Charles actually loved his wife quite deeply, but it just wasn't his nature to give her the intimacy she desired. He was quite compassionate, however, whereas some people with a closed heart chakra can be judgemental, rejecting, or "hard-hearted." For Charles, relationships were an area where he felt painfully awkward, but he did the best he could. It was understandable, however, that he preferred to keep his focus on his academic work, where he could excel and gain recognition.

Sandra, his wife, was more on the excessive side of the heart chakra. She was afraid to be alone and found her identity in the reflection of others. She often gave too much, with the hidden agenda of wanting to receive approval. She led a busy social life, always running off to a meeting or a gathering of friends. She was heavily involved with her children (sometimes to the point of meddling), and constantly felt rejected because of her husband's lack of relationship skills.

Relationships often exhibit opposites like Charles and Sandra. It's actually a perfect combination for each partner to grow towards the other – in this case for Charles to learn how to be more relational and intimate, and for Sandra to become more self-reliant. While they were polarized, however, they were caught in a vicious cycle. The more Sandra tried to get Charles' attention, the more he retreated into his work. And the more Charles retreated, the more Sandra tried to make up for her loss with her busy social life.

As we worked together over a period of months, Charles began to learn the language of relating and became more able to express his feelings, while Sandra learned to interpret his behaviour as just a pattern he was working through, rather than a reflection of his love for her.

Excessive and deficient qualities in the fourth chakra

Excessive qualities	Deficient qualities	Balanced qualities
Need for attention and approval	Critical, intolerant	Empathetic, peaceful
Clinging to others	Isolating, withdrawn	Self-accepting
People pleasing	Uncaring	Caring, compassionate
Poor boundaries	Excessive boundaries	Generous
Co-dependency	Fear of intimacy	Forgiving

Further actions to open the heart

Love and compassion are necessities, not luxuries. Without them humanity cannot survive.
THE DALAI LAMA

We are all born wanting and needing love, but we are not born knowing how to create it. That must be learned, and perhaps all our experiences can be seen as teaching us about love. This may be the lesson of our times, as we shift from a largely third-chakra based society to one organized through the principles of the heart.[3]

The core of a relationship is the ability to relate through connecting what's inside yourself to what's inside another person. This is the basis of intimacy, which requires first knowing yourself, then loving yourself enough to feel safe being vulnerable. Loving yourself, you are less dependent on what others think of you, and that leaves more room to be authentic, intimate, and empathetic.

It's not just working with the body that opens the heart, but actions in day-to-day life. Generosity, compassion, caring, and forgiveness can all generate the opening of the heart. The result of these actions is joy, liberation, and peace.

- Where can you be more generous with those around you (or even to yourself)? That may be generosity with time, energy, or tolerance, as you soften your stance towards others.

---

3. For more on this concept, see Anodea Judith, *The Global Heart Awakens: Humanity's Rite of Passage from the Love of Power to the Power of Love*, Shift Books, San Rafael, CA, 2013.

- Where can you be more compassionate towards others (or towards yourself)? Can you forgive their foibles, knowing that you have your own?

- Where can you be more caring?

Quesada Gardens in San Francisco

You never know when a small selfless action will ripple out into the world and create change. In 2002, Jeffrey Betcher, a gay white male, decided to move into a predominantly black, crime-ridden, drug-dealing neighbourhood of San Francisco. Afterwards, he questioned his sanity, as cars would line up daily to do drug deals, and no one felt safe.

The central reservation of the road in front of his house was littered with car parts, dead refrigerators, and used syringes, but one day he came home from work to find that his neighbours, Annette Smith and Karl Paige, had planted some flowers in front of his house. Jeffrey decided to plant some flowers in return.

This produced a cascade of wonderful events. Within a year the whole community had replaced the weeds and garbage that had been the norm with fruit trees and bushes, vegetables and flowers. Neighbours came out to work together, getting to know each other and taking pride in where they lived. Crime and drug use declined, and a viable community rose up in their place.

At the time of this writing, the Quesada Garden Initiative has six community gardens, two murals and a neighbourhood coalition to spread this model beyond their own community.

Exercise: Giving and receiving

You never know what will be the long-term results of giving with no expectation of return. Here's a simple exercise to realize the joy that comes from serving others and the joy you can give to others when you allow them to serve you.

- Pick someone you know casually, like a neighbour, a friend, or a co-worker, and think of something special to do for them. Allow your imagination and creativity to take hold – what would be a nice delight? You could bake them some muffins, mow their lawn, or offer to take their kids to the movies. If it's a co-worker, you might just leave a card on their desk with a vase of flowers, take them to lunch, or buy them a small present. If you're standing in a store while someone packs your groceries, simply compliment them on their smile or their clothing, or appreciate the job they are doing for you. If you're at a tollbooth, pay the toll for the car behind you. Do it without expectation of return, and if you really want to up the ante, give your gift anonymously.

- Notice the way you feel watching or imagining the person discovering their gift. Imagine that they want to "pay it forward," meaning they are inspired to do something similar for someone else instead of needing to pay it back to you.

- Next, imagine something that someone can do for you. Maybe you need advice on a project, help with your kids, or a neighbour to help you plant a local area. Learn to ask for help and notice how it feels to receive it. You are giving a gift when you allow others to give to you.

POINTS TO REMEMBER

- The heart chakra is in the centre of the chakra system and represents balance and integration between polarities of above and below, mind and body, heaven and Earth, masculine and feminine.

- The heart chakra is related to the element air and can be accessed through the breath.

- Opening the chest leaves more room for the breath, which in turn creates spaciousness in the body.

- A child comes into the heart chakra stage as they master impulse control and become socialized.

- We develop a social identity that is designed to create approval and acceptance from others. Accepting ourselves takes the burden off others and allows authenticity and vulnerability.

- We open the heart through selfless actions of generosity, compassion, and forgiveness.

- The result of an open heart is joy, expansion, and connection between the inner and outer worlds.

Chakra Five

SOUND

Chakra Five

Sound

If you want to find the secrets of the universe,
think in terms of energy, frequency and vibration.
Nikola Tesla

Location:	Neck, shoulders, jaw
Name and meaning:	Visuddha, purification
Purposes:	Communication, harmony
Elements:	Sound, ether
Principles:	Truth, resonance, harmony
Developmental age:	7–12 years
Identity:	Creative identity
Orientation:	Self-expression
Demon:	Lies
Right:	To speak and be heard
Seed sound:	*Ham*
Colour:	Bright blue
Balanced form:	Truthful, creative, expressive

The realm of vibration

Welcome to the etheric realm of the throat chakra! Here we tune in to the element of sound, carried on the air of our breath. Our mouth shapes our breath into words, guided by our thoughts and our will. But there are also subtler vibrations streaming through our body, and indeed through all of life, with communication happening in each and every cell. The fifth chakra invites us to witness this vibrational level and listen deeply to the rhythms and sounds that express all that is within us and around us.

From the primordial "Om" at the heart of creation, vibration ripples through all of existence. Scientists have found that everything is vibrating, down to the smallest subatomic particles that make up our cells. In fact that rapid vibration is what makes the world seem solid, even though it is mostly empty space.

When consciousness receives the ripples of vibration, communication occurs. Our body is an instrument that is constantly vibrating with all that it receives, shaping our world, connecting and creating. We join the grand symphony of creation with our unique voice, singing the truth of our heart.

These vibrations emanate from our being into the field around us, mixing with other people's fields of vibration and the field of the environment. They become part of the auric field, that subtle field of energy that surrounds our body. Did you know that this field is constantly vibrating, singing out the sum total of all the vibrations within you? We unconsciously experience this whenever we meet someone. We even say, "I really resonated with this person" or "I didn't like his vibes."

When we resonate with someone, there is a desire to stay in connection. When there is disharmony, we want to break away so we can return to that resonance within ourselves. Noisy environments, full of traffic noise, phones ringing, people yelling, or even aeroplane noise, are all tiring to the body. One reason we need silence and sleep is to return to our internal resonance, which happens by itself when we are no longer bombarded by invasive sounds.

The purpose of the fifth chakra is to find this internal resonance among all the subtle vibrations within, to live in harmony with others, and to know, speak, and live our truth.

Understanding the fifth-chakra symbol

The symbol of the throat chakra is a lotus with 16 petals that contains a simple downward-pointing triangle, the *Trikuna* of the goddess Shakti, which is still rising up into spirit. The 16 petals represent the 16 vowels of the Sanskrit alphabet. (The rest of the alphabet is on the other chakra symbols, excluding the crown.) It is said that vowels are the expression of spirit, whereas consonants are the form spirit takes in matter. So the throat chakra is the entry point into pure spirit. Just as the neck connects the head to the body, so the realm of sound infuses spirit into matter.

The animal is the elephant Airavata, sometimes depicted with seven trunks, one for each chakra.

The seed sound is *Ham*. We will discuss seed sounds more fully later in this chapter.

The purifying nature of sound

Three things cannot be long hidden: the sun, the moon, and the truth.
BUDDHA

The element of the fifth chakra is *sound*, and this chakra relates to communication, listening, learning, creativity, and self-expression. When we communicate, we are vibrating our breath into words that have meaning, connecting our inner consciousness to the awareness of another with some bit of information. Communication allows connection and makes it possible for consciousness to dissolve its boundaries and be shared by many.

The vibrations of sound have a subtle effect on matter and a profound effect on spirit. Evelyn Glennie, a deaf percussionist from the UK who writes and conducts entire symphonies, claims that she "hears" sound by feeling the vibrations through her body. She often plays barefoot to feel the vibrations coming up through the ground as she keeps in time with a whole orchestra. She has recorded several albums and is inspiring to hear in concert. She even sings!

The name of the throat chakra, Visuddha, means "purification." Coherent sound that is harmonious and resonant has a purifying effect on matter. When sound is played so that it vibrates a flat metal disc with salt on it, the vibrations move the salt crystals into mandala-like patterns. Change the sound, and the shape of the mandala changes as well, but with any pure sound, it is always ordered and centred. So sound has an effect on our bodies as well, and new research is exploring the potential of sound waves to heal illnesses and restore vitality.

In a similar way, speaking our truth, while it might be messy in the short run, has a purifying effect on everything. Truth has a field we can resonate with – it's something we can palpably feel. Even when the truth is difficult, it serves to liberate us in the long run. On the liberating current, moving up from the chakras, the truth will set us free.

People love to be around communication that resonates with them. That's why crowds flock to hear speakers talking about things they believe in, why politicians can create whole movements with passionate speeches, and why the audience cheers when the band plays that classic hit that everyone knows best. Resonance brings harmony to all our subtle vibrations and helps us feel whole and connected.

And lastly, the idea of purification through the throat chakra states that we must purify ourselves in order to access the transcendent realms of the upper chakras. As energy moves through the chakras from gross to subtle, we refine our vibrations at each chakra. The throat chakra – the narrowest part of the body along the core – makes vibrations subtler and subtler, preparing the mind for the stillness that takes us into non-dual consciousness in the sixth and seventh chakras. More about that later!

Tuning your instrument

All truths are easy to understand once they are discovered; the point is to discover them.
GALILEO GALILEI

We started this book with a simple exercise to help bring your chakras into alignment. Remember that you can think of them as jewels along a luminescent string of energy running between heaven and Earth – the inner cord of your soul. When you stretch out that luminescent string, you are tuning it up, just as you would tune a guitar string by stretching it between two points. If it is adjusted to the proper tension, it makes a beautiful sound. If it is too loose or too tight, it won't vibrate at its true frequency and the sound will be sharp or flat.

Life will most certainly pluck that string. And when it does, the string will vibrate with the impact. Under natural circumstances, that vibration will continue until the strength of the impact is cancelled out – usually a few moments. If the string is plucked harder, the sound will be louder and the vibration last longer. If it is plucked softly, the sound will be barely noticeable and the vibration last only a few seconds.

When life "plucks our string" with anything that has an impact on our soul, we naturally want to talk about it, cry about it, sing about it, or write poetry about it. If someone bumps into us on the street, we might say "Ow!" If an event at work impacts us during the day, we want to discharge its energy when we come home at night, perhaps by saying to a friend, "You'll never guess what happened to me today!" or discharging passively by zoning out in another conversation, or television, or a book.

Recently, while travelling, I heard about an area of California near where I live being consumed by wildfires, including Harbin Hot Springs, a spiritual centre for the whole Bay Area and a place I had frequented for many years. I felt grief-stricken and noticed I needed to talk about it to anyone who would listen, even though I was far from home and no one around me was familiar with the area I was talking about. But just being able to talk about it helped me deal with the sense of loss and devastation.

The act of expressing what has impacted us is natural and normal. When we do so, it leaves us in a state of balance. However, it's not always possible to express our truth. Sometimes we have no one to talk to. Sometimes, as is often the case with children, we are not believed or listened to. We might be ridiculed for what we are saying. If we're at work, it might be inappropriate to share our feelings, and we have to lock down on that inner vibration that wants to come out.

Our whole body is an instrument that the Divine is constantly playing. Blocking its natural vibration deadens the life within us and blocks our throat chakra. When we can't speak our truth, that vibration is stored in our body, and over time that body becomes dense, thick, or rigid – in a sense, "frozen." Rigid tissue does not vibrate very easily, and we lose the resonance with our own being. Over time, the natural resonance of our subtle vibrations fall into dis-harmony, or dis-ease.

It takes considerable effort to keep an important vibrational impact from being expressed. It's as if we have to post a sentry guard at the gateway of our throat chakra to keep what's inside from coming out. Unfortunately, that sentry guard isn't all that smart. It can't sort out what is OK to express and what isn't. It checks everything that comes through, even our creativity, our natural self-expression, and the strength of our voice. Much like going through a security checkpoint at an airport, this slows everything down and makes it more difficult for us to communicate. It takes us out of resonance with the world around us.

The demon of this chakra is lies – the opposite of truth. Anytime we're not fully telling our truth, we're living a bit of a lie. And remember, we can lie with our words to others, but we can also lie to ourselves, lie with our actions, our body, or our facial expressions. As children, we might have been the receiver of lies, or been part of a family that was living a lie. This demon can take many forms, but its antidote is the same action that opens your throat chakra: to speak your truth, to listen to others when they speak their truth, and to live in harmony with greater truths. This will enhance your creativity and allow you to be more fully present in your conversations with others.

Exercise: Finding your power song

If you watch young children playing freely, you will see that they love to move and make noise at the same time. They might rock back and forth from one leg to another and hum, or repeat a phrase in a sing-song-like manner. Looking closely, you will notice there's a strange kind of rhythm to it, and that the body and the sound are perfectly coordinated. In this exercise, you are invited to open to this playful freedom to find your power song.

- Find a place where you can walk freely and make a noise without feeling ridiculous. Your living room is fine if it's big enough to stride around in, otherwise find a place in the woods or on a beach where you can be alone. (Alternatively, you can do this exercise with others, so none of you feels silly.)

- Begin walking and allowing random sounds to come out of your mouth that reflect the rhythm of your walking. Any sounds will do: rhythmic humming, nonsense words, even phrases if they come to mind, maybe sounds like "bo-eem-oh-wep, bo-eem-oh-wep" or "in di baba, in di baba, ooh, ooh." Of course these are just examples, and you'll have to find your own!

- Once you loosen up and find a rhythm, begin to walk more purposefully and powerfully. Bring some energy into your legs and make each step deliberate, yet still allow yourself to move rhythmically and let the power flow through your whole body.

- As your steps begin to express your power, allow your sounds to mirror this power. They may change from your original sounds. This should happen organically, without effort or the mind getting too involved. Let it arise spontaneously.

- Continue walking powerfully until your sounds begin to find a groove and be repeated: this is your power song. Allow it to settle into something simple that you can remember and repeat when needed.

- Once you have found your power song, slow down your steps but continue singing your power song and notice how it feels in both your throat and your third chakra.

- Remember this sound. Perhaps even write it down. Next time you need a little extra power, mentally review your power song, or, even better, take a power walk and sing!

Mantras

The word *mantra* means "tool for the mind." Mantras are abstract sounds that are repeated over and over again. They are like advertising jingles, and we all know what it's like when an advertising jingle or a piece of a song gets stuck in our mind. Most of us find it annoying, yet advertisers know just how to infuse a thought into our brain so that we'll remember to buy their product.

Mantras are often used to instil a particular sound into our brainwaves and consciousness. They are tools to steady the mind for meditation. By focusing on a single sound that has little or no particular meaning, the mind stops running around in its usual chaotic way and becomes single-pointed.

Mantras also produce a subtle vibration that wakes us up in a way similar to an alarm clock waking us up from slumber. They are gentle vibrations designed to wake up the inner aspects of deities, virtues, or the chakras.

In the ancient texts on the chakras, there is a Sanskrit symbol at the centre of each chakra symbol. These represent the sounds that are said to awaken the energy or element of that particular chakra, called "seed sounds" or *bija mantras.* (We have mentioned these sounds briefly in the descriptions of each chakra symbol.)

The seed sounds are all listed below, and are followed by an exercise showing you how to work with them. However, the throat chakra is the chakra of creativity, so let yourself experiment and find your own way. You might even find that different sounds affect *your* chakras, since we are all different instruments, living in different bodies!

- Chakra one: *Lam*
- Chakra two: *Vam*
- Chakra three: *Ram*
- Chakra four: *Yam*
- Chakra five: *Ham*
- Chakra six: *Om*
- Chakra seven: *Silence*

Working with mantras

Now let's look specifically at how to use these sounds to activate your chakras. There are a variety of ways:

- You can use one sound at a time, silently uttering the mantra of a particular chakra in a state of meditation to make deeper contact with that part of yourself.

- You can chant the sound out loud or chant it with others, which is even more powerful.

- You can repeat all six sounds rhythmically, one after another, silently or out loud.

- You can use the sounds to send healing energy into different parts of the body.

- You can make patterns with the sounds, perhaps working on two or three chakras at a time or sending energy from one chakra to another.

Exercise: Chanting the *bija mantras*

- Sit cross-legged and begin opening your throat to sound. Make any kind of sound that wants to come out: big sounds, little sounds, words, humming.

- Now begin with the mantra for chakra one: *Lam*. Begin with just the first consonant and the sound that it makes, *luh*, and notice what happens in your body as you say it aloud. Then add the rest of the word and repeat *Lam* for at least one minute. (That's probably longer than you think!) Close your eyes as you do this and imagine your root chakra at the base of your spine pushing down into the Earth.

- Next move your attention up to the second chakra. Play with the *vuh* sound and feel what it does to your body. Now add the rest of the sound and repeat *Vam* for a minute.

- Then move your attention to the third chakra and play with the *r* sound of *Ram*. Add the rest and repeat as you did in the first two chakras. Notice the effect.

- Move your attention to the fourth chakra, working with the *y* sound. Think of the words that start with this sound: "yes," "yippee," "yay" – they are all happy words! Repeat the full *Yam* for a minute and imagine your fourth chakra pulsing with the sound.

- Move your attention to the fifth chakra. Play with the *h* sound and feel it come through your throat. Then add the full *Ham* and repeat it for a full minute.

- Next move to the sixth chakra, in the centre of the head, at brow level. Imagine light pouring into this chakra as you slowly chant the sound of *Om*. Allow it to be the full sound, which is *ah-oo-mm*, and repeat for one minute.

- Now that you have made the first six chakra seed sounds, sit quietly and focus on your crown chakra. Do not make any sound at all, simply listen to your body and notice the effects of this practice.

Developmental stage of the fifth chakra

Ten-year-old Kenny couldn't stop talking. From the time he came home from school to the time he went to bed, he wanted to share every detail of what he was learning, what his teacher had said, and what every one of his friends had done that day. His parents usually let him drone on with occasional nods and "mm-hmms," but they didn't really engage with him or ask questions. Kenny was wanting to connect through communication, and his constant talking was a way of trying to get not just attention, but the kind of communication that helps a child sort out what they are experiencing. When that communication occurs, children settle down and will often get quieter. Without it, they might drone on forever, not even hearing themselves when they speak.

Once a child becomes socialized and feels accepted by those around them, they enter the fifth-chakra stage of communication, a stage of immense learning and expansion of horizons. It's natural for children to want to express themselves, as it helps them process what they're learning. Ideally, our schools and family should foster that curiosity, with good communication that helps children understand the world around them and discover the truth within themselves. Much of that discovery comes through communication. "What are you feeling right now?" "What does that mean to you?" "What do you think about that?" Asking questions can point consciousness to what is inside and help that consciousness learn to express itself. Of course, it's very important to listen to children as well, to understand and be interested in what they're saying, and to validate their reality.

Unfortunately, many families and school systems fail to reach out to children in this way. The old adage that children should be seen and not heard shows that adults have not always been interested in what's really going on inside a child. Children may spend their early years being told to sit up and speak up, but when they get to the stage where they should be developing their throat chakras, they're often told to sit down and shut up!

Having to be quiet and sit still at school at an age when we should be out playing in the yard and making noise teaches us to override our natural impulses to express ourselves and to contain our energy instead. That's probably a good thing, otherwise as adults we'd be blurting out anything that came into our head at any moment. But in most cases, this containment goes too far and we learn to block our fifth chakra.

Since this developmental stage is also one of immense learning about the world – through discussion and

questions, books, films, the internet, movies, and school
– shutting down the fifth chakra can create learning
difficulties, or simply turn off the natural curiosity that
keeps a mind open.

Exercise: Communication in your family

Here are some more questions to review. Take a moment to reflect
on their truth, then write about them in your journal. For extra credit,
discuss these issues with a sibling or another family member and
compare notes on your childhood environment.

- How was communication in your family? Was it yelling and
  screaming? Silence and withdrawal? Did you see issues being
  discussed and brought to resolution, or were things shoved under
  the carpet?

- Did anyone ask you about your feelings and challenges and help you
  come to understand how to deal with them?

- Did you feel safe speaking your truth?

- Were you listened to when you did try to speak up?

- If you could have spoken your deepest truth at the time, what would
  you have said and to whom would you have said it? What would you
  have wanted to hear in response?

Creative identity

Creativity is allowing yourself to make mistakes. Art is knowing which ones to keep.
SCOTT ADAMS

Kenny is now developing his *creative identity*, which is oriented to *self-expression*. If his lower chakra development has gone well, he will have a sense of security (chakra one), connection to his emotions (chakra two), autonomy and confidence (chakra three), and self-acceptance from being loved for who he is (chakra four). With these chakras as solid support, he will then feel free to express and reveal himself, to ask questions and receive feedback, to explore the arts, and to dare to live creatively.

As adults, our creative identity may be that of an artist, a musician, a healer, a cook, a teacher, or a lawyer. It's the way we identify with our personal form of creative contribution.

What is the medium through which you best express yourself? What is the medium through which you best learn? Of all the expressive arts, which ones really communicate with you? Do you love to dance, go to art galleries, listen to music? You may find that you receive best from music, but express yourself through cooking or parenting or building things. How we listen and how we speak are not always in the same medium, but they are both part of our creative identity.

Excess and deficiency in the fifth chakra

Wise men speak because they have something to say;
fools because they have to say something.
PLATO

When it comes to communication, too much and too little
are usually pretty obvious – at least to everyone else. We
all know people who talk too much. They tell us every
irrelevant detail and run on and on. They try to keep people
engaged in what they are saying, but more often they turn
them off instead. This is an excessive throat chakra. (If
there were a 12-step programme for this, it would be called
"On and On Anonymous"!)

We also know other people who rarely speak at all, or, when
they do speak, have voices that are so quiet we have to
strain to hear them. I see this all the time in my workshops.
Such people often sit in the front row, and when they speak,
I can barely hear them, let alone the rest of the class. Once
I asked someone to speak up so the others could hear her
question too, and she promptly said she'd rather not speak
at all! That's a deficient throat chakra.

The question is *why* do we talk too much or too little?

Keeping quiet may be a lifelong result of not being heard,
of being ridiculed, or of believing that we can't handle the
"charge" that communication might bring, whether that
charge occurs within us or the other person. Sometimes
the charge in our own body can be so intense, it feels as
though everything that's unexpressed wants to run out of
the gate at once. Because that's too scary for most people,
they shut down the throat chakra even more. If you've

ever experienced a sudden lump in your throat when you've started to speak, coupled with a rapid heartbeat and sweaty palms, you'll know what I mean. Even though there's a deep desire to express yourself, the result is even more constriction.

To free this up, it's helpful to go to a place where you can freely make sound and just let as many sounds out as you possibly can: loud sounds, angry sounds, sad sounds, happy sounds. The more sounds you release, the less pressure you will feel in your throat, and the easier it will be to say the words you really want to say.

I have described how we have a natural tendency to express whatever impacts us. Energy that comes into the body is expressed back out through several channels: the feet, the arms, the mouth, and the genitals. If any of the other channels are blocked, the mouth may have to work overtime, creating an excessive fifth chakra. Talking is a way to discharge energy that can't be discharged elsewhere. It may work to a certain extent, but it's not really discharging the issues at their core. As a result it needs to be done again and again and can become a habit.

Excessive and deficient qualities in the fifth chakra

Excessive qualities	Deficient qualities	Balanced qualities
Talking too much	Fear of speaking up	Clear, concise communication
Excessive loudness	Speaking with a small, weak voice	Speaking with a resonant, full voice
Stuttering	Having difficulty putting feelings into words	Knowing your own truth
Gossiping	Being secretive	Being a good listener
Difficulty containing yourself	Being overly self-contained	Being in harmony with self and others

Expressing yourself

Do you ever have conversations inside your head, either as a rehearsal for something to come or as a way of talking to yourself? No, you're not crazy or hearing voices. This is a natural process that goes on inside everybody's head. It's how we sort things out internally, how we think things through. However, unexpressed truth takes up room in the fifth chakra, like a background noise that makes it more difficult to hear. If we're busy running conversations through our head, we're not fully listening to what's going on around us. As a result we're not in synch with others, nor resonating with them. If there is too much internal chatter, we can begin to live in a world of our own. Listening is essential to tuning our instrument, just as musicians listen carefully when tuning their instruments to those of others. This is why quieting the mind is helpful for deeper listening.

Here's a little exercise to do if you notice yourself drifting apart from someone you are otherwise close to, like a dear friend.

Exercise: Expressing withholds

Look inside for whatever you might not be saying to the person. Maybe you don't want to hurt their feelings, maybe you don't want to reveal yourself, maybe you just haven't had time to really connect deeply to them. Maybe there's an unfinished conversation in which you didn't get to speak your full truth.

Whatever you haven't said is called a "withhold." It's a piece of your truth that you've been withholding from someone for any of the reasons mentioned above. Most often it's the negative things we hold back, but sometimes we just forget to say that we've appreciated something or are too shy to say that we care. Of course, some of these things might be better left unsaid, yet still they are taking up room in our throat chakra and creating distance between us and the other person.

Step one

- Write down in your journal all the things you haven't said to the person. Don't mince any words. Express your truth in any way that feels authentic – it's your journal and no one but you is going to read it. Write down everything, until nothing more wants to come out.

- Notice how you feel getting these things off your chest. If you have been feeling negative towards that person, you might start to feel more positive once the negative things have been expressed. Write down the positive things as well.

- Here are some examples:

  - I didn't tell you how annoyed I was because the dishes were left in the sink last night.

  - I've been feeling lately that I can't talk to you.

  - I haven't really told you lately how much I love you.

- I wish you would hold me more/spend time with me/listen to me/apologize...

- I was annoyed when you ignored me at dinner the other night.

- I wish you wouldn't watch so much television.

- I want to spend some quality time with you.

Step two

After writing these things down in any way they want to come out, imagine yourself actually saying them to the other person. What would it feel like to say those things? Notice this is just an imaginary conversation where you get to see your own projection of your listener's experience.

Step three

Find a friend who will receive these withholds for you. Use the following script for this process:

- Your friend says, "Tell me something you are withholding from Patrick," and you say, "Patrick, I was really annoyed when you were late for our meeting."

- Your friend then says, "Thank you. Tell me something else you are withholding from Patrick."

- You then say something else, repeating the process until everything about Patrick is fully unloaded.

Note that your friend does not question, analyse, counsel, give advice, or comment. They only say, "Thank you and tell me something else you have withheld from..."

Step four

If possible, share your withholds with the actual person. I say "if possible" because that person may no longer be alive, they might live far away, or they might be unwilling to participate in such a dialogue. If they are willing, however, there is also a script to keep the dialogue contained:

- Begin with an enquiry before blurting anything out, for example: "Honey, I notice I have some things I haven't told you and they are creating distance between us. Would you be willing to hear them?"

- The answer might be "Yes, I would," or "No, I wouldn't," or "Not right now, I'm tired, can we set up a time later?" This answer must be respected. There is no point sharing your withholds with the actual person if they are not willing to participate in the dialogue. If they refuse, be content with steps one, two, and three.

- If the person *is* willing to listen, ask them to agree to reply simply: "Thank you. Tell me something else you have withheld from me." It's important that the person receiving the withholds refrains from defending, commenting, blaming, arguing, or interrupting. These withholds may be true or false from their perspective, but that's not the point. The point is to get them off your chest.

- The person you speak to may, in turn, have withholds they want to share with you. If so, repeat the same process, merely saying, "Thank you," after each one and listening fully.

Helpful hints

- Avoid blaming, criticizing, or attempting to state what the other is feeling. These statements usually start with the word "you," for example: "You always ignore me and act rudely. You're so angry all the time."

- A better way to share withholds is to use the "I" voice, for example: "Last night I felt invisible and so I got annoyed at the tone of the conversation. I was afraid I had done something to make you angry." This way the person can hear your experience, rather than a criticism.

- After the withholds, it's good to share something positive. This usually happens by itself after the negative things have been shared, but just in case, always sandwich your difficult communications with statements that are positive and encouraging. Examples might be: "I am really heartened that we've been able to have this dialogue, as I treasure our relationship and want to be closer to you" or "I do appreciate how much you clean up and take care of the kids. It really helps me a lot."

- And it's always nice to end with a hug and a smile.

POINTS TO REMEMBER

- The fifth chakra relates to sound, communication, self-expression, and creativity.

- Ninety per cent of good communication is listening.

- Mantras are sounds designed to wake up consciousness with their subtle vibration. Each chakra has a seed mantra used to activate its energy.

- Whatever we have withheld from someone tends to create distance.

- Holding back our truth creates density and even disease over time.

- The purpose of the fifth chakra is to harmoniously find, speak, and live our truth.

Chakra Six

LIGHT

Chakra Six

Light

*You have to find what sparks a light
in you so that you in your own way
can illuminate the world.*
OPRAH WINFREY

Location:	Centre of the head at brow level
Name and meaning:	Ajna, command centre
Purposes:	Seeing, intuition, wisdom
Element:	Light
Principles:	Luminescence, radiance
Developmental age:	12 years and above
Identity:	Archetypal identity
Orientation:	Self-reflection
Demon:	Illusion
Right:	To see
Seed sound:	*Om*
Colour:	Indigo
Balanced form:	Clarity, inspiration, vision

Lightening up

We've now made it through much of our chakra journey. We have grounded ourselves in earth in chakra one, sending our roots down deep. We've moved through the waters of emotion and sexuality in chakra two, learning to tune in to sensation and desire. In chakra three, we found our power and fired it up with our will. In chakra four, we breathed the air of love into our heart, then learned to speak our truth in chakra five. The next step takes us into the radiant glow of the sixth chakra to discover the luminescent light of the soul within. Here is where we enhance our intuition, develop insight, light our way, and find clarity, vision, and wisdom.

The sixth chakra is about seeing in the deepest sense of the word. What does it mean to really see – to not only notice the finer details around us, but to see within? Seeing plays a big part in what the mystics call "realization." To "realize," we must learn to see with "real eyes." That means piercing through the sixth chakra's demon of illusion to the eternal shining light of the life-force.

Light makes it possible to see, which is why it's the element associated with chakra six. Seeing where we are, we can navigate along our path, comparing the map to the territory. Our intuition becomes a subtle guiding force, and we gain perspective on the past, see what lies ahead, and choose our direction. Seeing clearly, we get the "bigger picture," and create meaning for our life through a guiding vision. This informs our decisions and tells us where to go.

Back in the seventies, I lived off the grid in a land-based alternative community. I loved every minute of it – being immersed in beauty and nature, tending a garden, planting trees, and conducting sacred ceremonies that honoured the seasons. I would never have left that simple paradise except for the fact that continuing to stay there didn't serve my vision of bringing the chakra system out into the larger world. I made the decision to return to the city for a while to go back to school, get my advanced degrees and write my first book, *Wheels of Life*. I chose my path according to what served my larger vision, even if it meant sacrifice in the short term.

Drinking in the light

Most of us are separated from natural light, spending time indoors, within walls, with a roof over our heads, getting outside for at most a few moments while we walk to our car or the bus. Our only light is artificial. But natural light is essential to health. We are missing an important "vitamin" if we are light-deprived. There is even a name for the syndrome suffered by people in far northern or southern parts of the globe, where the days get very short in the winter: Seasonal Affective Disorder, or SAD, which can lead to depression. Research has shown that even moderate exposure to natural light during those times can "lighten" up our mood.

Here's an exercise to help bring colour and light into your internal world:

Exercise: Depositing light into your inner temple

- Whenever you see a particularly bright colour, stop and focus on it fully. Really take it in through your eyes. Imagine breathing it in.

- Then close your eyes and see if you can remember exactly what you were seeing. If you cannot remember it clearly, open your eyes and drink it again. It is as if you are "depositing" that colour into your internal palette.

- Repeat until you feel you can create the colour within yourself.

You can also do this with light in general, though you should never look directly at the sun. Sometimes I'll see light glaring off a windshield, filtering through a tree, or sparkling in a sunset, and will also bring this light into my interior.

Exercise: Visualizing the inner flame

A further technique is to meditate in a dark room with a candle flame in front of you. Take the light of the flame in through your eyes until you can close your eyes and still see it clearly on the inside.

Through doing this practice over time, I've found that my dreams have become more colourful, my ability to imagine and visualize has become stronger, and I often see a soft inner luminescence when I close my eyes in the dark.

Understanding the sixth-chakra symbol

After increasing the number of petals on the chakra symbols from four to six, 10, 12, and 16, we now suddenly have only two petals in chakra six. My sense of this has always been that the two petals represent our two physical eyes and the circle represents the third eye, the psychic organ of perception.

Within this circle is the Trikuna of Shakti once again, connecting spirit and matter, and within it is the symbol of Om, the universal symbol of spiritual unity. Above the Trikuna is a shining crescent moon, signifying the pure white colour that is often seen when the third eye opens to the luminous light within.

It is said that the dualities of the figure-eight nadis, *Ida* and *Pingala* (*discussed on page 23*), meet in the sixth chakra and collapse there into non-dual consciousness. It is only in this state of single-minded focus that we rise up to the seventh-chakra state of pure awareness.

Opening the third eye

Imagination is more important than knowledge.
ALBERT EINSTEIN

The sixth chakra is also called the third eye. This is a deeper organ of perception that exists between our two physical eyes. It relates to the pineal gland, the light-sensitive organ within the brain that is responsible for visions, dreams, and the cycles of sleep and waking. This gland was called the "seat of the soul" long before its role was understood in modern times. In some lower animals, as well as in the embryo, it is actually a third eye.

It took about three billion years from the first appearance of life on Earth for evolution to create eyes that could see. That's a long time to be in the dark before putting the lights on! Once animals could see, it was possible for them to move towards food or away from danger. They could see each other, see the world around them, and begin to work together.

We are now at that same point in our evolution as a species – just getting to the stage where we have enough information about our world to see into the future; just getting the technology that gives us electronic eyes to see across the world, through movies, television, and the internet; just getting long-distance communication, such as Skype, that lets us see who we are talking to.

We are also just getting to the point where the masses are learning to raise their consciousness, meditate, and develop their intuition. And while it may not be mainstream yet, many people are developing their psychic abilities and using clairvoyance to see energy and auras for the purpose of healing. Learning to see in this way is a huge evolutionary leap.

What is essential at this stage is that we create a guiding vision for where we are going on this planet, one that enables long-term survival and flowering into the future. Seeing the future enables us to plan. Perhaps it is no coincidence that saving our "planet" means that we have to really "plan it." My global vision is that we are here to create heaven on Earth, and the path through the chakras is the means of getting there.

If a global vision feels too big for you to wrap your head around right now, you may first need to create a guiding vision for your own life. Where do you want to go? What do you want to contribute? What catches your attention? What draws forth your passion and purpose? Your vision is the vehicle that takes you to the fulfilment of your life's purpose. How much time do you spend planning your next vacation compared to planning the rest of your life?

Exercise: Imagine your vision

- Is there someone you admire who is living their vision? What inspires you about that person?

- What do you daydream about when your mind is idle? Is it something you would like to create in your life?

- If money were no object, what would you do with your life? Where would you give back to society from your good fortune?

- Imagine you are lying on your deathbed looking back at your life. Are you happy with what you've done with it?

- Imagine your family is gathered around your deathbed and you tell them you are ready to leave your body because you've fulfilled your life's purpose. What was it? What did you do? What effect did you have?

The command centre

People are like stained-glass windows. They sparkle and shine when the sun is out, but when the darkness sets in, their true beauty is revealed only if there is a light from within.
Elisabeth Kübler-Ross

Chakra six is called Ajna, meaning "to perceive" and "to command." The perception part is easy to understand – it's what happens when we open our eyes: we perceive what's around us. But that's only half of what the sixth chakra does. It also forms pictures in our mind that begin *to command* our reality. Like a stained-glass window, these internal pictures are the first thing that consciousness hits as it journeys down into manifestation. Not that we always get just what we visualize. Usually blockages along the way distort the image we hold in our mind. Still, our internal pictures and beliefs direct our attention and begin to bring our thoughts into form.

Most people think of seeing as something that happens passively: you just open your eyes, and images pour in. But it is also an active practice when you use your imagination.

That's how you "see" what you want to create – even though it doesn't exist yet! And the more actively you use your imagination, the better you get at creating what you want.

If you want to change or create something in your life, begin by visualizing it *as if it were already happening*. If you want to create more prosperity, daily visualize your bank account with a higher balance, or imagine landing the perfect job, or "see" all your debts paid off. If you want to create health, imagine sending light or colour to an ailing part of your body. If you are looking for your soul mate, imagine having a conversation with the perfect person, waking up together, or walking down the aisle to seal your vows of commitment.

A word of advice

Be mindful of the pictures you create about your life – either for yourself or others. Do you dwell on positive or negative images? Do you look in the mirror and focus on the extra fat around your belly, or do you see the beauty of who you are? Do you look at others and focus on what they are doing wrong, or reflect their positive qualities back to them? Kings and queens wore crowns of jewels that were beautiful because they reflected the light. When you learn to reflect the light of others, that light is magnified. Learning to see and enhance the good is a daily spiritual practice.

Colour and chakras

Colour is an aspect of light that brings essential frequencies into the body. Research has shown that people heal faster around green growing things, that blue has a calming effect and red is invigorating. And of course the chakras are commonly associated with colours reflecting the seven colours of the rainbow, from the lowest frequency of the visible spectrum (red), through orange, yellow, green, blue and indigo to the highest and fastest frequency, which is violet. If you want to stimulate a particular chakra, it can be helpful to surround yourself with its particular colour.

Exercise: Colour meditation

After you read this meditation, close your eyes for a moment. You might even consider recording it so you can be guided through it.

As your eyelids lower down to your cheeks, shutting out the light, imagine you are bringing light to the inside of your temple. You remember what light looks like from your process of drinking it in! You can recreate this light within your mind any time you like.

Now imagine that light shining down upon you from above your head. See it as a pure white light, as bright as you can possibly imagine, the colour of starlight.

Now imagine that your body is a prism that breaks up that white light into seven different frequencies of colour, one for each chakra.

As the light comes down upon your crown, imagine it becomes a bright violet, its light colouring the thousand petals of your crown chakra lotus.

Then imagine you go back up to that white light and pull down a ray of deep indigo blue, drawing it into your sixth chakra at the centre of your head, like a star sapphire, glowing with blue light.

Next bring down from that infinite white light a ray of bright turquoise, drawing it into your throat chakra. Imagine waves of vibration bathed in this blue emanating 360 degrees from your throat chakra.

Now reach up into that brilliant white light and bring down a beautiful rich green – the green of plants and forests. Draw that colour in with the breath and fill your heart chakra with it.

Now reach up into the pure white light to pull down the yellow ray, the colour of fire, energy of the sun. Allow your third chakra to expand and fill with bright yellows and shimmering golds.

Keeping all these colours in each of your upper chakras, reach up to the white light and pull down the colour orange, visualizing your second chakra filling with the warmth and energy of this colour. Feel it soothing and melting your body.

Finally, reach up through all the colours to that infinite white light and draw down a deep and vibrant red, the colour of your root chakra. Imagine you are sitting upon a red lotus whose four petals point in the four cardinal directions, flooded with red light. Allow that red to flow down your legs into your feet and into the ground.

Now see if you can visualize your entire inner core as a rainbow of light, each frequency vibrant and bright, illuminating your entire chakra system.

Notice if some of the chakras are brighter than others, and bring some extra light into the ones that feel closed down or dark.

Imagine these seven colours glowing like jewels at your deepest core, and the surface of your body surrounded by a luminous pale light encompassing you.

Record any impressions you want to remember in your journal.

Exercise: Seeing from a distance

When you change perspective, you see things differently. This is why getting out of town or creating a "change of scene" can help you solve problems and find new solutions. Here's a little exercise to develop your inner seer and perhaps learn something about yourself. You might be surprised by seeing some things you normally don't see at all.

Close your eyes and imagine you are rising up out of your body and floating at a distant point above your head, maybe in the upper corner of the room or even outside above your roof.

Imagine that you are looking down at yourself, watching yourself go through a typical day. See yourself waking up, brushing your teeth, eating breakfast, interacting with your family, going to work, and so on, all the way through to coming home and going to bed. See it as if you were watching an old movie or a YouTube video taken from a hidden camera.

What do you notice about yourself from this perspective that you don't see when you're in the middle of your day? You might notice that your posture slumps or that you don't open to as much love as there is available for you. I often notice that I forget to let spirit guide me and think I have to do everything myself. Others notice that they try too hard, or don't try enough, or that they are more frightened than they need to be.

Look at your characteristics with detachment and do your best to refrain from any judgement. Just "see" yourself as if you were watching someone else – but be intensely curious.

Then open your eyes and record what you saw in your journal. Don't give yourself advice, just write down what you saw.

Am I dreaming?

Who looks outside, dreams; who looks inside awakens.
CARL JUNG

Dreaming is an important part of the sixth chakra and of consciousness in general. It brings the unconscious forwards as images and conversation, so that the conscious mind can perceive it and make sense of it.

Even if you don't remember your dreams, research has shown that everyone dreams at night, usually several times. Each person has intermittent periods during sleep when the eyelids flutter, called REM (Rapid Eye Movement) sleep. You can even see your dog doing it sometimes! If you wake someone up as soon as they enter REM sleep and deny them their dreamtime, they will get increasingly unbalanced emotionally. So your dreams really are doing something, whether you remember them or not.

However, making a practice of keeping a dream journal is a good way to signal to your unconsciousness mind that you really are interested in what it has to say to you. Once that message gets through, you will find that you remember your dreams more readily. Even if you only remember a fragment of a dream, write that down and take some time to ponder it later.

As you record your dreams over time, notice if there are particular themes that emerge. What are you, the dreamer, typically trying to do in the dream? Where are you frustrated? Where are you rewarded? Look at every aspect of your dreams as an aspect of yourself, even if you dream about a car, or a flower, or a house. If you don't understand an element of your dream, conduct a little dialogue with it in your journal, asking its purpose. You may be surprised at what you learn.

Archetypal identity

The contents of the collective unconscious are archetypes, primordial images that reflect basic patterns that are come to us all, and which have existed universally since the dawn of time.
CARL JUNG

Archetypes are patterns in the collective consciousness – ideal images that are like blueprints for the myriad forms we experience. For instance, I can say the word "cat" or "mother" and it has a general meaning for everyone, even though each cat or mother is quite unique.

Learning to think in terms of archetypes is part of seeing the bigger picture. It's how we see ourselves reflected in what's unfolding around us. We might see the role that we're playing at work or in our relationship, or the role that others play in our life. Understanding these roles can free us to consciously choose the role we are playing or to let go of it. This is all part of the liberating current. Let me give you an example.

Thirty years ago, I was a busy woman. I was mothering four kids at home, administering a full-time psychotherapy practice, serving as president of a large organization, finishing graduate school, and my first book, *Wheels of Life*, had just come out. I found myself exhausted and sometimes confused over where to put my priorities. I look back now and say, "No wonder!" but at the time I sought out some Jungian therapy to help myself deal with these demands. In one of my sessions, my therapist asked me, "How come you're so over-identified with the positive aspects of the Great Mother?" In a flash of understanding, I realized (saw with real eyes) that I was trying to be a type E personality – Everything to Everybody. In doing so, I had taken on an archetype that was completely unrealistic. With that one simple question, my therapist busted the whole complex and set me free to be more authentically myself.

Maybe you now realize you played the Black Sheep in your family, or you were always the Good Girl or Good Boy. Maybe you felt you had to save everyone and played the Hero. Maybe you've been the Ghost or the Martyr.

Archetypes have both light and dark sides. Your own mother may have been a Withholding Mother or a Nurturing Mother. Maybe your father was an Angry Father or an Overprotective Father. Maybe it was your brother who played the Shadow in the family and you had to be the Good Girl to balance it out. And maybe you are denying the shadow in an archetype you are playing – just as I was denying the shadow side of the Great Mother.

Below are just a few of the roles we often play in the archetypal realm. How many do you recognize? You might also come up with some of your own.

- Mother
- Father
- Lost Child

- Good Girl
- Good Boy
- Lover
- Artist
- Healer
- Martyr
- Victim
- Hero (trying to save the world)
- Trickster
- Comedian
- Helper
- Rebel
- Teacher
- Builder

What role are you playing now? Ask yourself whether playing that role serves the situation the way you would like. If it does, then how can you really own that archetype and play it even better? If it does not, how can you let go of its grip and free yourself to live more authentically?

Sometimes just realizing what is happening is enough for someone to free themselves from a role; other times it requires giving yourself permission to do something different. For me in the story above, it required not only the realization of which archetype I was living, but also learning to say "no," even if it displeased someone at times. That's a skill I'm still working on!

Childhood stage

Children are naturally psychic and imaginative. They can make up entire scenarios in their play with dolls or soldiers. They may have imaginary playmates, or have a fine-tuned sense of other people. Unfortunately, this sixth sense often gets shut down as we grow up. Few parents or teachers know how to foster these abilities in children, because they never had a chance to open and develop these realms.

After the creative identity of the fifth chakra has set in, from the age of seven to 12, the archetypal identity begins, in the pre-teen and teenage years. Now a child is asking why at an entirely different level, using their imagination to see life differently. There is a deep need to belong, to have an archetypal identity – whether it's as a gang leader, a teacher's pet, or the class president. The pre-adult begins to imagine life a different way, to comb their hair into spikes or tattoo their body, or become obsessed with an archetypal image like a movie star.

We must make sure we do not stamp out a child's imagination or a teenager's need to experiment with these archetypal and tribal identities. It's part of trying out different realities, and part of the way we learn to see multiple possibilities. In a world that is rapidly changing, our ability to see in new ways is of paramount importance.

What is unfortunate is that young people are not usually provided with meaningful archetypes, such as those in the myths and legends of heroes, gods and goddesses. Instead, what they get is stereotypes, which are less satisfying.

If we wish to help counter this, reading mythology, playing with the images on a Tarot deck, or working with astrology are all ways to begin to think archetypally.

Excess and deficiency in the sixth chakra

George and Jennifer were an odd pair. She had a childlike innocence and lovely round eyes that were wide open. She was interested in everything spiritual – past lives, chakras, auras, crystals, you name it, while George was about as cynical as you could get. It was amazing how they managed to live together, yet they clearly adored each other.

Jennifer was excessive in her sixth chakra. She could imagine anything and believed that whatever popped into her mind represented something real. She really was quite visionary, and she had strong psychic abilities, picking up on subtle cues from other people and then making interpretations from them. But she was largely untrained in these matters, and she couldn't sort truth from fiction in the many images that she perceived. She had an excessive sixth chakra.

Her husband was grounded and practical, with a stout body and a loving sense of humour. He had little use for much of Jennifer's fanciful imagination, but he found it amusing and would gently tease her about it. He had never seen such things himself, so he didn't believe that any of it even existed. He tended towards deficiency in his sixth chakra, and was perhaps a little excessive in his first-chakra grounding.

Despite these differences, this couple managed to be happy together. They could still see and appreciate each other's beauty without expecting the other to have the same outlook on life.

Excessive qualities	Deficient qualities	Balanced qualities
Hallucinations	Lack of imagination	Imaginative
Delusional	Difficulty visualizing	Insightful
Obsessive	Insensitive	Intuitive
Nightmares	No dream recall	Remembers dreams
Intrusive memories	Denial (blind to truth)	Clarity
Difficulty concentrating	Poor memory	Visionary

The demon of illusion

Since this chakra is about seeing clearly, the demon is illusion. When we get stuck in any kind of illusion, it obscures our vision and clarity. I've seen anorexic women who thought they were fat. I've seen people fantasize about a relationship with someone who had no interest in them. I've seen people firmly believe that their next investment was going to make them rich, only to lose all their money. History has shown that humanity has been deluded many times. It has happened to all of us, and when the illusion is shattered, it is often a rude awakening.

Illusion can take the form of denial – refusing to see what's there. It can take the form of distortion, seeing something different from what is apparent to everyone else. It can even take the form of full-blown hallucination when it is more severe. Yet to the person infected with the illusion, what they see seems absolutely true and real. How do we know when we are suffering from the "false seeing" of illusion?

This is where communication comes in. Sometimes it's helpful to get a reality check. Ask a friend or two if they think you are deluded when you tell them about what you see. Constantly question your beliefs and assumptions. Eliminate your expectations as much as possible. When you no longer expect something to look a certain way, you can better see things the way they really are.

The sixth chakra is where duality becomes integrated. If you see something as either all good, without any shadow at all, or entirely evil, without any good, chances are you aren't seeing clearly. To see something in its wholeness, including yourself, you must understand that every light casts a shadow, and every shadow creates contrast that heightens the light.

POINTS TO REMEMBER

- The sixth chakra is related to the element of light and the ability to see and gain insight.

- Natural light is important to health. When we spend too much time indoors, we become light deprived.

- The pineal gland is a light-sensitive organ in the centre of the head that is responsible for sleep, dreaming, and visions. It functions best when there is a natural rhythm of light and darkness.

- The demon of this chakra is illusion, which keeps us from seeing clearly.

- This chakra relates to the archetypal identity – the role we play in the bigger picture of our life.

Chakra Seven

CONSCIOUSNESS

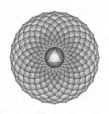

Chakra Seven

Consciousness

*No problem can be solved from the same
level of consciousness that created it.*
ALBERT EINSTEIN

Location:	Crown of the head
Name and meaning:	Sahasrara, thousand-fold
Purposes:	Awakening, understanding, enlightenment
Elements:	Thought, consciousness
Principle:	Awareness
Developmental age:	Early adulthood and beyond
Identity:	Universal identity
Orientation:	Self-knowledge
Demons:	Attachment, ignorance
Right:	To know
Seed sound:	Silence
Colours:	Violet/white
Balanced form:	Awareness, presence, intelligence

Consciousness, the final frontier

Humans have a distinct ability for highly sophisticated consciousness. The ability to feel, touch, see, hear, and smell is based on a consciousness that is capable of perceiving incredible detail about the world. The ability to remember, to think and plan, to simply be aware, is also a miraculous thing.

Consider all that your consciousness can do – recognize countless voices on the telephone, follow the directions to hundreds of places, know how to do a myriad of things, to speak, to remember, to create. That you can decipher these shapes of ink on a page and turn them into meaning – that alone is a miracle! And this is only the tip of the iceberg of what consciousness is and what it can do.

Thirteen billion brain cells make all that possible, and the number of connections between them is greater than the number of stars in the universe! We literally carry the universe inside us, for all that we perceive and understand comes through our consciousness. But do you know that the mind is 100,000 times more sensitive to the *inside* of the body than to the outside, with far more sensory receptors for *inner* cues? No wonder the mystery of consciousness is uncovered from deep within.

In the seventh chakra, we explore that mystery. Our final step on the chakra journey takes us to the underlying essence that has been running the show all along. Here we look beyond what we see or hear to the faculty beneath our seeing and hearing that makes it possible to do that.

What is that faculty? How does it work? Where does it come from? Who feels the world through your senses?

Who thinks and plans and perceives our reality? What is a thought? What is intelligence? What is awareness? What is mind? What is this mysterious non-substance that runs through all of creation? These are the kinds of questions we ask as consciousness turns its attention towards exploring its own nature. Questioning is one of the ways it awakens.

Understanding the seventh-chakra symbol

The crown chakra is also called the "thousand-petalled lotus." To the ancient yogis, each of the chakras was a lotus that blossomed with the awakening of consciousness. But the thousand petals of this chakra implies that this lotus is infinitely blooming. Indeed, as we reach the higher end of the chakra spectrum, we reach into the infinite nature of the cosmos and universal consciousness. Here there are no limits.

The challenge of the crown chakra is for our consciousness to remain centred in the exact middle of the lotus, even as the myriad petals of reality bloom incessantly all around us. Can we remain centred and still in the midst of traffic noise, people yelling, challenges at work, and the many losses and impacts that occur daily? This requires detachment and a deeply grounded inner peace. Seventh-chakra practices, such as meditation, are designed to hone this skill. Here we transcend the usual things that "hook" us in life and learn to breathe and just be. Attachment, as the demon of this chakra, may keep us from frolicking in the infinite.

The programming of consciousness

We are what we think. All that we are arises with our thoughts. With our thoughts, we make the world.
BUDDHA

If you think of your body as your hardware, with bones, muscles, and organs, then your mind is your software, programmed with the languages you speak, everything you have learned, and all your memories and beliefs. The life-force energy we have been discussing all along is the electricity running through the computer, enabling the hardware and software to connect.

In a computer, the programming in the software tells the little electrons where to go and where not to go in the hardware, and that creates what you experience on your screen, whether you're watching a movie, analysing data, or reading an email. If your computer's battery goes dead, for example, it doesn't matter how many programs you have installed or whether you have bought the latest hardware on the market. It's useless until you have a current running through the system again.

In the same way, your life-force energy connects your mind to your body. The programming in your mind tells your energy where to go in the body and where not to go. It tells you to pull in your stomach if you think someone is looking at you, or to keep quiet when someone else is speaking. It tells you when to take action and when to be careful. It is behind all the myriad things that guide your behaviour, from childhood and cultural programming to chosen beliefs and values. The way you eat, treat others, and pursue goals are all a direct result of your programming, both conscious and unconscious. It directs your life-force into and out of each of your chakras, all according to how your programs interpret the situation.

Your programming might be working well – you may have a program for getting fit or accomplishing goals – or it might be working against you – you may have a heart chakra program that leads to failed relationships or a first-chakra program that keeps you in poverty. Here at the seventh chakra, the task is to examine the programs that run your life and get the bugs out of them, so they can better do what they're supposed to do, whether it's protecting your survival, developing your power, creating intimacy, or helping you be creative.

In the computer analogy, *consciousness* is not the software/ mind or the hardware/body, but the *user* of the whole system. It's my consciousness that is typing these words right now and your consciousness that is reading them and making sense of what they are saying. My consciousness might look at what my computer is doing and say, "I don't want it to do that. I want it to do this instead!" Then I "operate" on my computer by typing a different command, going to a different website, or shutting the whole thing off and turning my attention elsewhere. In the same way, your consciousness can "operate" on your mind by examining your programming, changing your beliefs, and creating new ones. You can get the bugs out of your programs so your life runs more smoothly. Humans might be the only species that can do this!

Your programming is the prime director of your attention. If you believe that a TV show is going to be interesting, you give it your attention. You're reading this book right now because you believe that chakras are worth studying!

Paying attention

Attention is a valuable resource. Wherever you invest it, that's where you'll get your return.
ANODEA JUDITH

Attention is an important facet of consciousness, and the one we are most familiar with. Right now, you are focusing on reading these words, but maybe other things are vying for your attention – your phone might be ringing, or your kids might be making noise, or your stomach might be growling, turning your attention towards food. You walk down the street and every sign or storefront is hoping to grab your attention. Throughout the day, there are millions of things that distract attention.

Whatever our attention is focused upon creates our *experience*. If I look outside my window right now, I have an experience of a grey, cloudy day and the gentle hum of a plane flying overhead. If I put my attention on my body, I notice I'm sitting forwards in my chair and that it's a bit chilly in my office this morning. If I look back at my computer screen, my body and the outside landscape slip into the background and my attention returns to the ideas I am trying to convey.

Our attention is like the browser we use to surf the internet. Wherever it is pointed, that's what comes onto our screen. Change our search, and we change the information coming to us. Change the focus of our attention, and we change our experience.

Gaining control of our attention is one of the first steps to mastering our mind and opening the gates to higher consciousness. In fact, being successful at anything requires the ability to keep our attention focused on whatever we're doing, despite all the distractions.

Meaning and beliefs

It's not the events of our lives that shape us, but our beliefs as to what those events mean.
Tony Robbins

We have stated that attention creates our experience. But then what does the mind do with that experience? It tries to make *meaning* out of it. It does that through interpretation.

Right now you are turning these squiggly black shapes into words that have meaning. If you were looking instead at a complex mathematical formula, or an alphabet in a strange language, the shapes might not have any meaning for you. Similarly, when you listen to someone speaking to you, you make meaning out of their words. You interpret them as meaning they love you or are angry at you. You might decide this means they are your soul mate or are no longer worth your attention. It's all in the interpretation.

From the day we're born to the day we die, we create meaning out of our experiences. We take little bits of meaning here and there and over time add them together to create beliefs. If our mother is burdened with too many children and is cross with us one day, we might think it means we've done something bad. If we have that experience frequently, those meanings might add up to the belief that there is something wrong with us or that we are unlovable. It's rare that a child has the perspective to see that their parents are challenged. Most children form the belief that it's their own self that's flawed.

Beliefs are formed from our interpretations of our experience. Later they actually govern our interpretations and therefore our experience. If you believe you aren't smart enough, you'll look for evidence to prove that you don't have what it takes. If you believe life is hard, well, guess what? You'll see all the places where life is hard.

Beliefs are structures of consciousness the way bones are structures of the body. When it's said that beliefs create our reality, that's partly true, because they direct our attention, which creates the reality of our experience.

We have thousands if not millions of beliefs. They govern everything we say and do. One of the tasks of the seventh chakra is to examine them.

In the computer analogy, beliefs are the "operating system," which is the part of the software that interprets all the other programs on a computer. Beliefs tell us how to operate in life, and, like any operating system, they need to be upgraded from time to time, especially when they aren't bringing us the reality we want, or when they don't match the reality we have. But first we need to know what they are.

Exercise: Exploring your beliefs

Start by doing a little journal-writing on your beliefs about the major areas in your life and see what they might say to you and about you. What do you believe about:

- *Chakra one:* Your body? Your finances? Your sense of safety and trust in the world?

- *Chakra two:* Your sexuality? Other people's sexuality? Your emotions? Your desires?

- *Chakra three:* Your right to have power? Your purpose in life?

- *Chakra four:* Finding and keeping love? Being in a relationship?

- *Chakra five:* Your creativity? Your ability to communicate?

- *Chakra six:* Your psychic abilities? Your ability to achieve your dreams? Your imagination?

- *Chakra seven:* Spirituality? Religion? Connection to the Divine? Meditation?

Notice whether those beliefs serve you or impose limitations. If you feel a particular belief is limiting you, write down a belief that might be more constructive for you.[4]

Meditation isn't what you think

> *When there are thoughts, it is distraction; when there are no thoughts, it is meditation.*
> RAMANA MAHARSHI

It is early morning, cold and dark. I climb out of bed and make a cup of tea to warm myself up. Then I sit, holding the cup in my hands.

At first my mind is restless, thinking of all the things I have to do today. I drink the tea as my mind wanders through the remnants of sleep and dreams still clinging to my consciousness.

Then I put the tea down to begin my meditation. I settle into my seat, spine erect. I begin to regulate my breathing – slowly in, slowly out... Sometimes I'm impatient for the wave of inner peace that comes over me in meditation. *Come on, bliss, I don't have all day!* I think to myself. But then ideas begin to surface. I start to remember.

---

4. For more about diagnosing and changing beliefs, see Anodea Judith and Lion Goodman, *Creating on Purpose*, Sounds True, Boulder, CO, 2012, or check out Lion's free material on beliefs on his website: www.transformyourbeliefs.com

I continue to sit very still, settling into my breath, inhaling more deeply as I draw the breath up my spine, exhaling for longer as I drop down and in. I silently intone my mantra, which has become so deep within me it produces deep waves of bliss.

Before long my thoughts become quiet. A soft light begins to glow in my inner temple. I forget about my breath. Peace washes over me as my breath and brainwaves knit together in deep resonance. Now instead of wanting to hurry, I want to stay here forever. Time passes without measure.

At some point it is finished, at least for now. I look at my watch. It might have been 10 minutes, it might have been an hour. I might have touched in briefly, just enough to reset my dials for the day, or I might have had the equivalent of a night's sleep just sitting on my cushion. It varies from day to day, but even if I touch this place for but a moment, it reminds me of what is real. This is meditation.

The oldest of techniques, tried and true for thousands of years, meditation is a balm to the soul. There is no activity better for gaining command of your attention, upgrading your beliefs, elevating your experience, and accessing the seventh chakra. Meditation takes your attention away from all its distractions, so you can experience the limitless realm of consciousness itself. It cleanses the mind, calms the body, refines awareness, and has lasting measurable benefits. It is one of the prime remedies to reduce stress and promote healing. If you only have time for one thing each day, find some time to simply meditate.

There are countless ways to do it. Some of them happen by themselves, such as when you're daydreaming while washing dishes or driving a car. Others involve intense forms of concentration, such as counting your breath or reciting scripture, while still others are as easy as taking a shower and imagining a stream of cosmic energy flowing through you.

I've heard that if you ride an elephant through the marketplace in India, its trunk swings wildly to and fro, knocking over stalls, stealing bananas, and generally creating havoc. But if you put a stick in the elephant's trunk, it gives the elephant something to focus on. The trunk is so busy holding the stick, it doesn't flail about.

In the same way, most meditation techniques are about giving your mind some kind of stick to hold so your attention isn't swinging from this to that. It might be a candle flame, a mantra, or a particular question. It doesn't really matter which you choose, because focusing on an object or question is just a technique to create a single-pointed mind. Once you learn to do that, you can gradually let go of the stick and your mind will be trained to settle into meditation easily at will.

Below are some common types of meditation. If you don't already have a meditation practice or technique, I suggest you try one of these and stay with it for a while. Meditation has cumulative results that might not be apparent after one or two tries. It's a practice, which means it takes time to reap its benefits. Be patient, and wherever you are restless or find your mind wandering, simply bring it back to your focus.

Types of meditation

Observing the breath
In this form of meditation you simply watch your breath go in and out of your body smoothly and evenly. If your mind wanders, you simply bring it back to your breath. Some people like to count as the breath goes in and out, making sure that it is even in both directions, or sometimes longer on the exhalation, which promotes relaxation.

Mantra meditation
Mantra meditation uses the inner repetition of a sound or phrase whose vibration is designed to wake up a facet of consciousness. You simply repeat the mantra over and over in your mind. Mantra meditation is one of the chief techniques of Transcendental Meditation. (*For more on mantras, see page 130.*)

Focusing on an image
Whereas a mantra is a sound, a yantra is an image. It might be an image of a deity, a teacher, a colour, or a chakra symbol, but whatever it is, it keeps the mind focused.

Pondering an idea, such as a Zen koan
A Zen koan is a riddle that has no logical answer, such as "What is the sound of one hand clapping?" Because it has no answer, it keeps the mind enquiring.

Observing the sensations of the body
In normal waking consciousness, we often ignore our body's sensations. Yet the body, as the unconscious mind, may

contain important messages. Focusing on its sensations allows them to be completed, eventually freeing the mind to frolic in the emptiness.

Directing the flow of energy in the body
Bodily sensations often have a flow or direction of energy. Once you detect that flow, your mind can learn to direct it to certain areas that need healing or to various chakras.

"Running Energy" is a meditation technique that simply directs energy through your body, either from the top down or the bottom up. Like taking a shower, the energy that runs through you cleanses you.

Listening intently to music
We listen to music all the time, but to really listen to a piece without doing anything else at all is a meditation in and of itself.

Sitting quietly in a spiritual place, such as a church, temple, or sacred site
Sometimes a place with strong spiritual energies can be a meditation. These sacred spaces invite us to be quiet, to open our mind and heart, and listen deeply to what is within and around us.

Deep states of prayer
Prayer is a kind of meditation in which we commune with the Divine by saying what is deep in our heart and then hopefully listening to guidance in return.

Studying holy texts or inspired writings

We are fortunate in the modern era to have access to myriad sacred texts from a variety of religions around the world. Spending time reading and contemplating the wisdom of ancient teachers can be a meditation.

Watching movements in nature, such as fire, water, or clouds

Sitting by the sea and silently watching the waves crash upon the shore, sitting by a fire and watching the flames dance, or lying on your back staring at the clouds are all ways to meditate in nature. These natural rhythms tend to be hypnotic, allowing the mind to go deeper.

Walking in nature

There are also walking meditations, where you take each step slowly and deliberately, truly noticing all that is around you. To be silent in nature is to feel the wind and sunshine on your back, to hear the birds and crickets, smell the flowers, and touch the essence of the Divine.

Developmental stage of the seventh chakra

When we quit thinking primarily about ourselves and our own self-preservation, we undergo a truly heroic transformation of consciousness.
JOSEPH CAMPBELL

The crown chakra has a less defined developmental stage than the other chakras, as it is always developing. It begins, however, with evaluating your life, questioning your assumptions and beliefs, examining your actions and motives, and learning to detach and look at things objectively.

Generally, this begins to happen as a child passes into young adulthood. Then they begin to form their own worldview, often questioning what their parents have taught them. They may choose their own religion, course of study, or path of experiences, in line with their soul's purpose. Supporting a child to take this step is essential. The world is changing so rapidly we can't possibly expect all our beliefs to remain the same.

Some people, however, don't get to this stage until midlife, and some never at all. If you have read this far in the book, then I'm sure you have already been searching and questioning for some time. My advice: don't hurry for an answer. Allow the questioning and searching to lead you deeper into the mystery. Often when we think we have an answer we stop our questing, and hence our learning.

Excess and deficiency in the seventh chakra

I travel widely, often visiting metaphysical centres and bookstores where people are interested in spirituality. I see all kinds of people and enjoy receiving their questions. And I often see those who are so intent on pursuing their spiritual path that they have ignored their body or their family, or simply don't have their feet on the ground. I remember one occasion when I was chatting with someone after a talk and a man came up and interrupted the conversation to tell me how he had already achieved enlightenment and permanently opened his crown chakra. I was too polite to say anything, but I wanted to say, "If you're so enlightened, then why didn't you notice you just rudely interrupted us, without any awareness of your impact?"

On another trip, I was teaching at a yoga studio run by two women. I taught there several days in a row and noticed only one of the women doing the work of opening the studio, cleaning, and taking care of all the mundane tasks that were involved in running the establishment. By the end of the week, I asked her where her partner was. She said, "Oh, she does three hours of spiritual practice every morning and can't show up for work until noon. She leaves it all for me to do." I detected a note of resentment, and reflected on how the woman doing the work was perhaps doing even more spiritual practice than her partner.

We live excessively in our crown chakra when our spirituality is ungrounded, when we don't take care of business or when we think that more meditation will solve everything. I once met a woman who had abandoned her three children to go and live in an ashram and another who fasted to the point of harming her body.

These are all examples of an excessive crown chakra, of using spirituality as an avoidance of other levels, sometimes called "taking a spiritual bypass."

Those who "live in their head" also have a kind of excessive crown chakra. Such people access everything through their intellect, avoid their emotions, and are constantly detached from the passion of life. While this detachment can serve a purpose, it's excessive when the person is overly detached from the body and from other people.

Since I am a spiritual teacher, I see fewer people on my tours who are deficient in the seventh chakra, but I hear about them. A woman will come up and ask me to sign her book and say, "I could never tell my husband about this. He's an engineer and would think I was crazy." Much of the world, steeped in scientific materialism and only believing in what can be measured and observed empirically, tends towards a deficiency in the seventh chakra. This can show up as cynicism about spiritual matters, subtle energy, and any form of connection with something larger that is unseen.

I also see a deficiency in the seventh chakra in people who are convinced they have the one true right and only way. They may have spiritual beliefs, but they have never questioned them and cannot entertain the possibility that anyone else's beliefs are valid. This, too, is a kind of deficiency, one in which a person is held back from the infinite by attachment to their beliefs.

Excessive qualities	Deficient qualities	Balanced qualities
Frenetic worship	Cynicism	Equanimity
Intellectualizing	Rigid belief systems	Open-mindedness, wisdom
Spiritual addiction	Apathy	Intelligence
Dissociation from the body, the world	Learning difficulties	Presence
Excessive purity, righteousness	Materialism, self-indulgence	Spiritual connection

Transcendence

When they have contemplated the world, human beings have always experienced a transcendence and mystery at the heart of existence.
Karen Armstrong

Ultimately, the goal of the seventh chakra is an experience of transcendence. When the mind is no longer focused on the particular, it can frolic in the infinite. This is the final goal of the upward liberating current: to free ourselves from all that limits us and experience the liberation that comes from letting go of attachment.

As the demon of the seventh chakra, attachment keeps us fixated on the particular. To the degree that we are attached to something – to a concept, to how we look, to what others think of us, to our youth, to being right, to having what we want – we are not fully free. Releasing these attachments frees the spirit from the ego and allows it to soar to the higher chakras. Released, we can better love, hear the truth, see clearly, and understand.

Transcendence is the ultimate state of consciousness. It is consciousness without an object, consciousness that is infinite, blissful, timeless. It is not even something that can be described. It can only be accessed through meditation, or sometimes intense experiences of life and death that transcend all our other mundane concerns. We might touch it briefly when we fall in love, or have ecstatic sex or moments of creativity, but it is courted through meditation.

Downloading the Divine

It is very hard to stay in the realm of transcendence all the time, however. At best, those of us who lead mundane lives get to touch these heights every now and then in deep states of meditation. Then we have to come back down and deal with what's around us.

When we truly meditate, we may find that there are instructions from spirit hanging out just above our crown chakra, waiting for us to be quiet long enough to listen to them. Our little brains have the capacity to download consciousness from its ultimate source – the infinite nature of the Divine, the source of all. When we empty out our minds, we have room to take in new information, and I call this "downloading the Divine."

After you have meditated, take some time to write in your journal, type on your computer, draw a picture, play music, or dance. You may find yourself inspired by something beyond your normal consciousness, by a kind of Grace that is moving through you. Ultimately, tapping the Divine is opening to that Grace, allowing it to flow through you, out of you, and into the world. In this way, you awaken the Divine within, and this is the purpose of working through your chakras.

POINTS TO REMEMBER

- The seventh chakra is about consciousness itself, and especially about becoming aware of our own awareness.

- In its mundane state, consciousness is always busy making meaning out of our experience. From that meaning, we create beliefs.

- Beliefs are structures of consciousness. They govern our experience.

- Questioning our beliefs opens our awareness to new possibilities and expands our crown chakra.

- Meditation is the prime technique for combatting stress, downloading the Divine, and developing our seventh chakra.

Putting It All Together

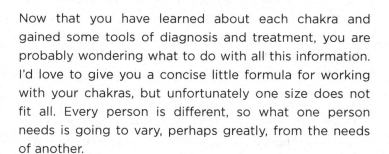

Now that you have learned about each chakra and gained some tools of diagnosis and treatment, you are probably wondering what to do with all this information. I'd love to give you a concise little formula for working with your chakras, but unfortunately one size does not fit all. Every person is different, so what one person needs is going to vary, perhaps greatly, from the needs of another.

Some people live in their heads and their growth will come from learning to bring their energy downwards into their lower chakras. Grounding would be a paramount practice, for them, along with paying attention to emotions and generating the vital energy of power.

Other people live in the practicality of everyday demands and may be very grounded by nature. Such people take care of business and make sure their survival needs are covered, but may not have as much room in their lives to frolic in the upper chakra realms of spirituality and meditation. The liberating current becomes more important here, the current most people think of when they talk about "working their chakras." Moving energy upwards will open the higher chakras.

If a client comes to me with a heartache because they've just lost a relationship, I work with their heart chakra. If they come in with power issues, or trouble communicating, I work with the third or fifth chakras respectively. However, I'm always looking at a more complex picture. Sometimes power issues result from not being grounded. Sometimes communication problems are more about standing in your power. Sometimes one chakra is compensating for something lacking in another chakra, either above or below. We are always living in the whole system – it's just a matter of how the energy is distributed. The goal is to find balance in your chakras, which will lead to balance in your life.

We have discussed how each chakra can become excessive or deficient. This simple diagnosis is based on whether you are too focused on a certain chakra-related area of your life or whether you tend to avoid that area. This diagnosis then tells you what you need to do. If you are compensating and focusing too much on one area, such as sex, power, or love, then you need to let go a little and redirect your energy to another chakra. Believe me, you won't lose what you have accomplished – but you will shore up the chakras that have been sacrificed in the meantime.

If you have diagnosed yourself as having a deficient chakra, then you need to pay *more* attention to that level of your life. Stop avoiding these issues and give them your attention. Open your body in those areas through yoga or exercise. Do some journal-writing about the topics of that chakra and see what comes out. Learn to receive energy in this area of your life.

When in doubt, I always suggest that you begin with grounding and work your way up. You can't go wrong with that tactic, and almost everyone I meet in this modern-day world could use more grounding.

It all begins with awareness. As you bring more energy into your body, notice where it goes, what feels good and what doesn't, what makes you feel alive and what drains you. Become keenly attuned to your energy system and that awareness alone will do wonders to set you on the path of awakening.

Use the exercises in this book, and if you are interested in following your path further into the chakras, see the resources at the end for further suggestions.

Most of all, be patient with yourself. Sensing energy and working with it successfully is a fine art that develops over time. Doing an exercise once won't make much of a difference, but having a regular practice will make a huge difference. Be diligent and persistent as well as patient.

The chakra system is a formula for your wholeness and a template for your transformation. It is a map you can use for the rest of your life. With the chakras as your guide, you'll find the journey just gets better and better each step along the way.

Resources

When I first began writing about the chakras, 40 years ago, there was very little available on the subject that was accessible for Westerners. Now there's a huge amount of material. Below you will find an annotated bibliography of some of my own books and a few that I recommend from other people whose work I respect. Know also that live workshops can give you a completely different experience than a book. You can find out about my live workshops and online telecourses at my website: **www.sacredcenters.com**

My books

Wheels of Life: A User's Guide to the Chakra System, Llewellyn Publications, 1987, 1999 (revised edition). Understanding the chakra system on a deeper level – its basic philosophy.

The Sevenfold Journey: Reclaiming Mind, Body, and Spirit through the Chakras (co-authored with Selene Vega), Celestial Arts, 1993. A basic workbook arising out of the popular nine-month chakra intensive workshops.

Eastern Body, Western Mind: Psychology and the Chakra System as a Path to the Self, Celestial Arts, 1997. This book goes deeper into the psychological aspects of each chakra, with more about their developmental stages, excesses and deficiencies, and ways to heal them.

Chakra Balancing, Sounds True, 2003. A multi-media kit including a 102-page workbook and two audio CDs with meditations and a yoga practice, and seven illustrated chakra cards, in a boxed set.

Contact: The Yoga of Relationship (co-authored with Tara Guber), Mandala Press, 2006. Points and postures for how the chakras play out in relationship.

Creating on Purpose: The Spiritual Technology of Manifesting through the Chakras (co-authored with Lion Goodman), Sounds True, 2012. This book takes the top-down journey through the chakras, with practical tips on how to clarify and manifest your life's purpose and create your highest dreams – on purpose!

The Global Heart Awakens: Humanity's Rite of Passage from the Love of Power to the Power of Love, Shift Books, 2013. A look at human cultural evolution in terms of the chakras that examines our rite of passage from the third to the fourth chakra.

Anodea Judith's Chakra Yoga, Llewellyn Publications, 2015. This book describes the relationship between chakras and yoga, with over 200 full-colour pictures of poses, breathing practices, yoga philosophy, mantras, and more.

Books by other authors

Thomas Ashley-Farrand, *Chakra Mantras: Liberate your Spiritual Genius through Chanting*, Red Wheel/Weiser, 2006. More than just about mantras, contains full chakra philosophy as well.

Arthur Avalon, *The Serpent Power: The Secrets of Tantric and Shaktic Yoga*, 1919, Dover Publications, 1974. Translations of Tantric texts on the chakras, with excellent commentary. Very esoteric and hard to read, but a classic book on the subject that was one of the first to bridge East and West. Keep your Sanskrit dictionary handy.

Alan Finger, *Chakra Yoga: Balancing Energy for Physical, Spiritual, and Mental Well-Being*, Shambhala Publications, 2006. Contains some basic poses organized by chakra with anatomical drawings, also an informative CD.

Sundar Shyam Goswami, *Layayoga: The Definitive Guide to the Chakras and Kundalini*, Routledge and Kegan Paul, 1980. Translations of the old texts, focusing mostly on mantra and yantra practices. Also descriptions of the lesser-known subtler chakras.

C. W. Leadbeater, *The Chakras*, The Theosophical Publishing House, 1927, 1997. The chakras from the Theosophical point of view. This book was one of the first published in English on the chakras and is a classic.

Karla McLaren, *Your Aura and Your Chakras: The Owner's Manual*, Samuel Weiser, 1998. The more psychic side of the chakras – working with the energy field using simple visualization and shielding practices.

Susan Shumsky, *Exploring Chakras: Awaken Your Untapped Energy*, The Career Press, 2003. This has some of the most accessible writing on the esoteric material on the chakras. Contains information on sub-chakras, layers of the Sushumna, and things you won't find anywhere else.

Heidi Spear, *The Everything Guide to Chakra Healing: Use your Body's Subtle Energies to Promote Health, Healing and Happiness*, Adams Media, 2011. A practical guide full of useful exercises and tips.

Videos

Seane Corn, Chakra Flow: An In-Depth Training for Energetic and Emotional Healing, DVD, Yoga of Awakening series, Sounds True, 2015

Anodea Judith, *The Illuminated Chakras: A Visionary Voyage into Your Inner World*, DVD, Sacred Centers, 2005. A 28-minute open-eyed meditation and visionary art journey with 3D animation and 5.1 surround sound. Languages: English, French, Italian, Spanish, and German.

Audio CDs

Dean Evenson, *Chakra Healing*, Soundings of the Planet, 2008

Jonathan Goldman, *Chakra Chants*, Etherean Music, 1998

Steven Halpern, *Chakra Suite: Music for Meditation, Healing and Inner Peace*, Inner Peace Music, 2010

Anodea Judith, *The Chakra System: A Complete Course in Self-Diagnosis and Healing*, Sounds True, 2000. An eight-hour CD audio series with instruction booklet.

—, *The Beginner's Guide to the Chakras*, Sounds True, 2002. A 73-minute CD.

—, *Wheels of Life Guided Meditations*, Llewellyn, 1987. A 70-minute CD available through www.sacredcenters.com

Layne Redmond, *Chanting the Chakras: Roots of Awakening*, Sounds True, 2001

—, *Chakra Breathing Meditations*, Sounds True, 2012

Robin Silver and Steve Gordon, *Chakra Healing Zone*, Sequoia Music, 2006

Sophia Songhealer, *Chakra Healing Chants*, Sequoia Music, 2003

Suzanne Sterling and Christopher Krotky, *Chakra Flow: Music for Yoga and Meditation*, Sounds True, 2014

Velez Glen, *Rhythms of the Chakras*, Sounds True, 2000

Acknowledgements

My 40-year journey across the rainbow bridge and back has embraced many travellers and guides along the way. My greatest teachers have been my students and clients, along with those healers who have helped me on my personal journey – too many to name.

In the publication of this book, I would first like to thank Amy Kiberd for reaching out to me with the invitation to write it, and further all the wonderful people at Hay House whose hands and hearts have been part of this creation: Elizabeth Henry for editing, Leanne Siu Anastasi for design, Julie Oughton and Lucy Buckroyd for seeing it through to publication, to the production team, to Jo and Ruth in PR, and to the Sales and Marketing team for their continued help and support.

I would also like to acknowledge Shanon Dean, administrator of Sacred Centers, not only for keeping the business together while I write, but for providing the illustrations herein.

And finally, to all my readers who dare to take this exciting journey to consciousness. May we meet someday along the rainbow bridge connecting heaven and Earth.

Anodea Judith
March, 2016
California, USA

ABOUT THE AUTHOR

Barbara Lance

Anodea Judith is the founder and director of Sacred Centers, a teaching organization that offers workshops and teleclasses in psychology, chakras, evolutionary activism, yoga, manifestation techniques, and much more.

She holds a doctorate in Health and Human Services, with a speciality in Mind-Body healing, and a Master's in Clinical Psychology. Her bestselling books on the chakra system, marrying Eastern and Western disciplines, have been considered ground-breaking in the field of Transpersonal Psychology and used as definitive texts in the USA and abroad.

With a million books in print in 17 languages, Anodea's books have won her the reputation of solid scholarship and international renown as a dynamic speaker and workshop leader. Her bestselling titles include *Wheels of Life* and *Eastern Body, Western Mind*.

www.sacredcenters.com

Free e-newsletters from Hay House, the Ultimate Resource for Inspiration

Be the first to know about Hay House's free downloads, special offers, giveaways, contests, and more!

 Get exclusive excerpts from our latest releases and videos from *Hay House Present Moments*.

 Our *Digital Products Newsletter* is the perfect way to stay up-to-date on our latest discounted eBooks, featured mobile apps, and Live Online and On Demand events.

 Learn with real benefits! *HayHouseU.com* is your source for the most innovative online courses from the world's leading personal growth experts. Be the first to know about new online courses and to receive exclusive discounts.

 Enjoy uplifting personal stories, how-to articles, and healing advice, along with videos and empowering quotes, within *Heal Your Life*.

Sign Up Now!

Get inspired, educate yourself, get a complimentary gift, and share the wisdom!

Visit www.hayhouse.com/newsletters to sign up today!

HAY HOUSE

Look within

Join the conversation about latest products,
events, exclusive offers and more.

f Hay House UK

🐦 @HayHouseUK

📷 @hayhouseuk

💜 healyourlife.com

We'd love to hear from you!